Thrive
In a HIVE

The Case for Experiential Entrepreneurial
Exercises in the Classroom

MONICA KNIGHT, PhD

A Wood Dragon Book

THRIVE IN A HIVE – The Case for Experiential
Entrepreneurial Exercises in the Classroom

Cover design: Callum Jagger
Interior design: Christine Lee
Author photo (back cover): Koren Bear

Published by:
Wood Dragon Books
Post Office Box 429
Mossbank, Saskatchewan, Canada S0H3G0
www.wooddragonbooks.com

Available in paperback and eBook
Paperback: ISBN: 978 1990 863 035
eBook: ISBN 978 1990 863 042

Author contact information
Email: monica@shosholoza.ca
Website: https://shosholoza.ca/

Dedication

This book is dedicated to my wonderful son Gregory who continues to dance his own dance.

I learned from Dr. Cyril Kesten,
who so artfully supervised my thesis work,
to take to heart the poetic Spanish phrase "*nadie te quita lo bailado*" that expresses that no matter what obstacles and criticism you encounter ...

no one can take away from you what you have danced.

Table of Contents

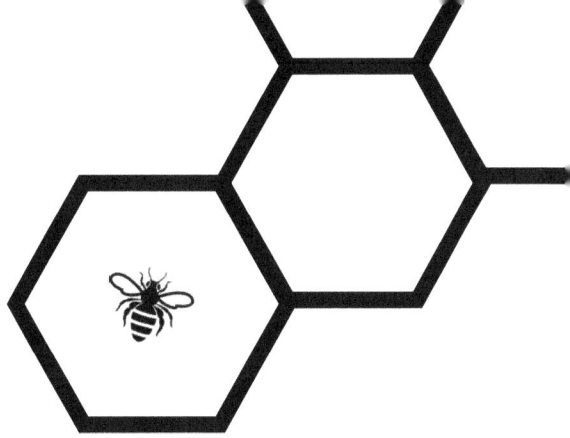

Introduction

Today's youth have become the most entrepreneurial generation since the Industrial Revolution. According to a 2009 report from the accounting and business management firm, Ernst & Young, as many as 5.6 million Americans under the age of 34 are actively trying to start their own business. Furthermore, E&Y reported that one third of new entrepreneurs are younger than 30 and more than 60% of people 18–29 years of age stated they want to own their own businesses.

With these explosive numbers comes a similar interest in the field and demand for entrepreneurship education.

Business educators have evolved beyond the myth that entrepreneurs are born, not made and even have embraced the idea that enterprise education should focus beyond only developing entrepreneurs.

Leading management thinker, Peter Drucker (1909-2005) said that there is nothing magical about the entrepreneurial mystique; it is not mysterious, and it has nothing to do with the genes. It is a discipline, and, like any discipline, it can be learned. Enterprise education in the K-12 system in North America, once commonly focused on developing entrepreneurs, has evolved to embrace the approach that not all entrepreneurship students need to be, or could be, entrepreneurs. Many students wish to be educated about all manifestations of the entrepreneur, entrepreneurial careers, and entrepreneurship—including what it is, how it works, and its contribution to society. This means that K–12 entrepreneurship classes should educate "for," "through," and "about" enterprise.

Educating "for," "through," and "about" diverts attention away from any specific economic interests or outcomes and directs attention towards the development of entrepreneurial thinking. Along with the benefits to economies, entrepreneurial thinking can be applied by students to any situation in life that requires the navigation and negotiation of unpredictability, the need for ingenuity and innovation in problem solving, creativity, flexibility, self-direction, and the ability to respond to widely different situations.

But learning entrepreneurship as a discipline, like mathematics, is not sufficient. Embracing the idea of entrepreneurial education for broad results is not sufficient either. Entrepreneurship has to be an emotional choice, one where passion lives, where the HEART of the entrepreneur combines with the ART of the craft and discipline.

This book is both the ART and HEART of entrepreneurship. The first part of the book explores my story as a serial entrepreneur. My HEART. Not only what worked, but what didn't and why—how

I learned to dance to the heartbeat of my own drum. The middle part of the book explores the ART of entrepreneurship and delves deep into the research and discovery from my master's and post-graduate studies and research. The final part of the book is written to help the reader take these concepts to HEART, to explore ways to take this material into the classroom, and to move towards success as an entrepreneur and/or teacher of intrapreneurship.

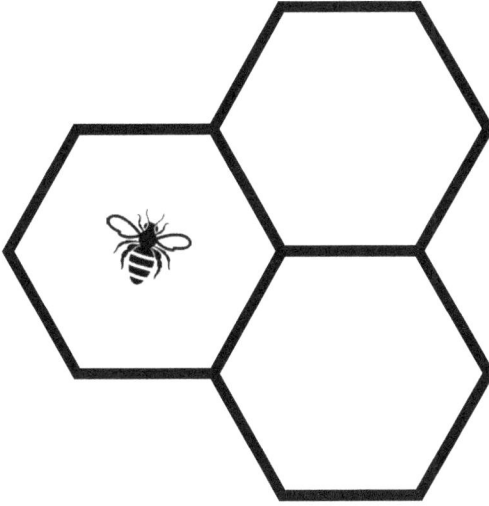

Part One

A Personal Journey of Entrepreneurship

In the form of an interview between the author and her publisher, this section explores Monica's entrepreneurial journey, what worked and what did not, and how she learned to "Thrive in a Hive".

————————————

WDB: Before we begin with how you became passionate about entrepreneurship, tell the readers why you decided to write this book and why now?

MK: Until 2003, I viewed myself as a practitioner of entrepreneurship and not a researcher of the subject. However, in the pursuit of my Master of Leadership thesis, I investigated a broad range of entrepreneurial activities practiced via cooperation and interdependence. Following on the heels of my master's thesis was my PhD dissertation work, which combined my previous research and my years of experience as an entrepreneur. The result of my studies, research and experience was the development of a supportive approach for K-12 teachers to introduce the process of entrepreneurship and the *art* of entrepreneurial thinking to their students. This book outlines the argument for experiential entrepreneurial learning in the classroom as well as details a series of experiential exercises for teachers to use with their students.

WDB: Prior to your research, you began to develop this set of experiential learning exercises to aid teachers in guiding students in entrepreneurship. Why?

MK: Teachers want students to become introspective and develop the independent thoughts and actions to wash off the disempowering thoughts of risk, failure, and the challenges of self-employment. Rather than one-off experiences for individuals, I promote long-lasting entrepreneurial behaviour in group settings, also known as *Intrapreneurship*, or *Thrive In A Hive*.

WDB: Can you be too old or too young to become an entrepreneur?

MK: The majority of self-employed people are over 35 when they become entrepreneurs and nearly 42% of the self-employed are over 45 when they jump into business for themselves. Some are much younger, and some are much older. Annette joined our enterprise in Gravelbourg at an enthusiastic 18 years of age and Maisie join Marmalade Cottage at a gracious 75. Generally speaking, by the age of 40 or so the habit of a regular paycheck, and the safety of health and pension plans carry enormous weight in any possible decision to strike out as an entrepreneur. Many people settle for running a prospective full-time business only as a part-time hobby in their garage or basement.

WDB: When someone jumps into self-employment later in life, is there a reason?

MK: People going through a major life event may yearn for the freedom and control that self-employment offers. A change in personal circumstances, such as a divorce or career downsizing will often prompt a move to self-employment. In my case, it was a geographical move that triggered my entrepreneurial efforts in Saskatchewan—I was removed from the corporate jungle of Johannesburg, South Africa with a population of 6 million and dropped into the rural environment of Lafleche, Saskatchewan with its population of 508 and few employment opportunities. I needed to create the opportunity to employ myself.

WDB: Is understanding business the most important thing to be successful as an entrepreneur?

MK: While analytical thinking is a superb foundation for business, it is the creative ability to visualize and conceptualize success that carries the entrepreneur through the loneliness of pursuing an entrepreneurial dream.

WDB: Are there personal characteristics that are requisites for success? And if so, what are they?

MK: Yes there are, but these personal characteristics have nothing to do with personality type—the real key is a strong work ethic that translates to a dogged determination to achieve the goal set, and the persistence to overcome any and all obstacles that may present themselves.

WDB: How can you know if you have the right stuff to be a successful entrepreneur?

MK: The entrepreneurial spirit is a mere glimmer inside some people, while for others it's a shining beacon. The energy that comes with the entrepreneurial spirit is often seen as a strong work ethic, and indeed it is. These inspired people don't put boundaries on how many hours they put in or how hard they'll work to achieve their goals. They know deep down that they will get there. To discover their capacity for business success, individuals should think about what they are willing to commit to for the first two years of their business and what they are willing to commit to long-term.

WDB: What are the characteristics a successful entrepreneur needs short-term?

MK: The willingness to make sacrifices, such as opening their business at times of the week, month, or year when others stay closed. They need to be willing to work for less money and benefits than any unskilled employee they might be employing. They might even need to be willing to distance themself from friends who do not encourage them.

WDB: What long-term characteristics does a successful entrepreneur need?

MK: They need to strive to finish what they start, set goals and work towards them with high levels of energy and stamina. They also need to be willing to take full responsibility for the profit and loss of the enterprise and to learn to move on from mistakes.

WDB: What is the first and best step to success?

MK: Your positive attitude is the first and best step to success. This contrasts with the belief of some fledgling entrepreneurs, who believe financial backing, is the first step. There is a belief in some that a start cannot be made without first having access to capital, financial backers, and a solid financial plan. I say having a strong work ethic, ambition and perseverance is more important!

WDB: So how important is money to success as an entrepreneur?

MK: They need to have the wealth or income to endure while their business grows. Sometimes I use the mantra "don't give up the day job!"

WDB: Do you have a belief system for success - a set of rules you live by?

MK: #1 - I will always budget my time like I budget my money. #2 - I will develop a bubble mentality where I closely focus on my ideas for my business. #3 - I will plan breaks and not become a workaholic. #4 - I will avoid the trap of perfectionism. #5 - I will not procrastinate. And #6 - If radical surgery on my business is needed, I will perform it, clean up the debris and move on with the remaining healthy parts. We all want our ideas to succeed and that is particularly true among entrepreneurs. But perfect information is never available at the outset of an enterprise, so adjustments are often needed. Sometimes, radical adjustments are needed. So, as the saying goes, "If you can't change the direction of the wind, you must adjust the sails."

WDB: Your company is called Shosholoza. What does that word come from and how does that relate to your concept of entrepreneurship?

MK: Shosholoza is a Zulu word that means moving on. The sound of it represents to me is the sound of the train wheels moving on the tracks. Sho-sho-lo-za. Sho-sho-lo-za. You can hear it. And moving on is essential as an entrepreneur—to be able to face setbacks and carry on.

WDB: When was your first entrepreneurial experience?

MK: In the girl guides while I was living in the UK. I was eleven. Our team was given the current day equivalent of $10 as start-up funds. We made fudge and sold our product on the playground. Within the time of one recess, we recovered the initial investment plus made the equivalent of $50 in profit.

WDB: So even from childhood, you began to develop an entrepreneurial mindset. When did you first become intrigued by entrepreneurship as a field of work?

MK: It really began to gain momentum in Africa. It's said that we all build resilience and tenacity through tough experiences. Such things as divorce, deaths of loved ones, job loss, forced retirement—and immigration. It's in these circumstances that many of us also contemplate self-employment. In India and then in Africa, I observed the spirit of cooperation, interdependence, and interconnectedness that proved that when many, with few resources, work together, they can generate collectively, what is called INTRApreneurship. In Africa, this is underpinned by "Ubuntu", which means "a person is a person through other people. "

WDB: You use the word Ubuntu to describe your entrepreneurial philosophy. What is Ubuntu?

MK: Ubuntu is the very heart of the hive system that I propose for entrepreneurship. In rural Africa, people survive through interdependence. Local women leverage scarce resources and integrate their diverse strengths to create viable micro enterprises. In these businesses, a strong foundation of common values is a prerequisite for success. The leader or group of leaders observe others, identify complementary strengths, form allies, and mobilize change. Psychological and self-assessment instruments designed to measure skills, knowledge, and personal attributes are unheard of in rural Africa. Therefore, common sense, wisdom and intuition must substitute in selecting participants for a hive. This pattern of the HIVE has served me well as I moved forward in practicing entrepreneurship and teaching it.

WDB: How is a HIVE different?

MK: Ubuntu values group solidarity, compassion, respect for human dignity, and collective identity—all which reflect the interdependence that makes the small business thrive in the HIVE. Given my understanding of the power of Ubuntu, in order for me to succeed at what I was trying to do in my little corner of rural Saskatchewan I had to help those around me to also succeed. Their success would enhance my success—that's Ubuntu. This is different from the North American concept which asserts that individual effort results in a personal sense of accomplishment and fulfillment. In the HIVE model, every entrepreneur and their individual businesses automatically contributes to the good of the entire pie. Each participant reaps the benefit of their personal effort through their business revenues, but at the same time their contribution makes the hive stronger, more vibrant for all.

WDB: You have said that Intrapreneurship is not the same as a cooperative or an incubator, but often these words are used by others to describe intrapreneurship. How are they different?

MK: Collaboration and interdependence can come in many forms. Cooperatives, incubators, and hives are all similar in that they require interdependence, but how they are structured and who has ownership and accountability are different. There is a strong understanding of cooperatives in western Canada and so often the HIVE model is misunderstood.

WDB: So how does a HIVE work?

MK Picture a Queen Bee business in the center and related business ventures surrounding her. The health and mentorship of the central enterprise builds an overall successful structure for the surrounding fledgling enterprises. The exercises in this book, and the ones I teach in workshops, instructs participants in understanding how to develop that HIVE structure, to work with cooperation and interdependence, and how to be a valid participant in the intrapreneurship within.

WDB: What was your first HIVE entrepreneurial adventure as an entrepreneur?

MK: I bought my first house in rural Saskatchewan for $1 and payment of the back taxes. Then I set about gathering fledgling entrepreneurs around me. My business HIVE was built around my business as the core. I was the experienced entrepreneur with enough income from the central business to pay the overhead expenses. The purpose was to help those gathered around the core business of the hive to experience low risk entrepreneurship. I wanted to spread the concept of Ubuntu that "if one grows we all grow "and the Zulu maxim "Alone you go fast, together you go further." In Saskatchewan, my first HIVE was *Marmalade Cottage* in La Fleche. This was followed by *The Renaissance Theatre* in Gravelbourg and *The 7 Wonders of Mortlach*, and *Shared Visions* in North Battleford and Wakaw. These entrepreneurial adventures were all in Saskatchewan. Then I ventured into Alberta with *The Red Barn* in Oyen, Alberta, operated by an interdependent group of entrepreneurs who named themselves The Belles of the Badlands.

WDB: You have said that goal setting is vital for an entrepreneur, whether the business is part of a HIVE or a stand-alone. Why do you believe that?

MK: Often the major obstacle that holds people back from their dreams and desires is the inability to create effective goals and execute them. With effective goal setting, the risk-and-reward rollercoaster is ridden with less angst—without sacrificing the joy of your big dreams. It's knowing where you are headed, where to focus your time and energy, and feeling in control to achieve what actually matters to you. That is why the exercises I developed in this program help fledgling entrepreneurs to set realistic individual and HIVE goals.

WDB: How is goal setting for entrepreneurs different than goal setting for things like weight loss?

MK: It is much more that a New Year's Resolution, it's more than saying you want to do something and writing up a plan. If you are goal setting for a business, it's a life plan—not just a business plan.

WDB: Why?

After the initial frenetic start up stage, many entrepreneurs feel as if they're adrift in the world, but goal setting is just as important after start-up if the business is to succeed long term. Business failures in the first few years are legendary—and there are many reasons for failure. Sometimes the business has reached a plateau or is declining. Entrepreneurs then feel like they are in an overworking rut with no escape and diminished returns for all those hours they put in. They work hard, with many days spent in a frenzy of activity but don't seem to get anywhere worthwhile.

Entrepreneurs have to be ready to learn and relearn, to be serious about reaching goals, and to want to change. Entrepreneurs can build confidence and create their dreams if they break down their goals into achievable steppingstones that keep them motivated to face the inevitable challenges that arise.

WDB: A person can have their financial situation in order, have entrepreneurial skills and attributes, but what if they simply are afraid of taking the leap and failing?

MK: Fear is part of human nature. As an entrepreneur, I face fear. The fear of failure can have a crippling effect on our ability to achieve. Luckily for us, there are plenty of ways to tackle this fear.

WDB: Such as?

MK: We can start by figuring out where fear comes from and re-framing the way we feel about failure. Ironically, previous success can be a cause of fear of failure; successful people like to win and achieve high standards. Certainly, no one enjoys failing, but when you have had previous successes, fear of failure can be so strong that avoiding failure eclipses the motivation to succeed. Insecurity about doing things incorrectly causes many people to unconsciously sabotage their chances for success. Fear of failure keeps you from trying, creates self-doubt, stalls progress, and may lead you to go against your values.

The main reasons why fear of failure exists are our patterns from childhood, our own perfectionism, over-personalizing with failure, or having a sense of false self-confidence.. For example, when it comes to childhood patterns, hyper-critical adults can cause children to internalize damaging mindsets by establishing ultimatums and fear-based rules. This causes children to feel the constant need to ask for permission and reassurance and they carry this need for validation into adulthood. But children can learn to re-frame beliefs about goals and success..

WDB: Is there any benefit in failing so you can move past the paralysis of fear?

MK: Having an 'all or nothing', 'win or lose', 'succeed or fail' mentality can leave us despondent, so failing helps us move past that polarity. For example, in companies that promote Intrapreneurship like Hewlett Packard, Microsoft and Pixar, people are actually encouraged to "fail early and fail fast." They encourage experimentation and innovation so that the core business can stay on the cutting edge. Luckily, the exercises later in the book addresses learning through failure as an entrepreneur. Practicing to fail creates further opportunities to succeed.

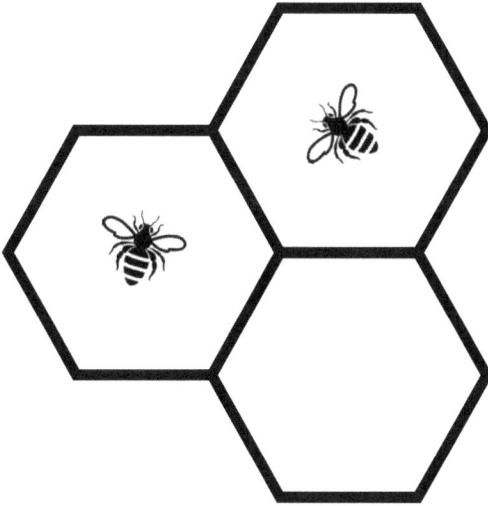

Part Two

A Case for Experiential Entrepreneurial
Learning in the Classroom

Chapter One

What is an *entrepreneur*?
What is *entrepreneurship*?
What is *intrapreneurship*?

The French root of the word entrepreneur comes from the term *enterprise*. The German equivalent is unternehmen, meaning to undertake. In the North American context, Merriam Webster dictionary defines an entrepreneur as *"one who organizes, manages, and assumes the risks of a business or enterprise."* The Commission of the European Communities offers the definition of entrepreneurship as "the mind set and process to create and develop economic activity by blending risk-taking, creativity and/or innovation with sound management, within a new or an existing organization."

The An April 27th, 2009 issue of *The Economist* magazine notes that Jean-Baptiste Say, a French economist, was the one who first coined the word *entrepreneur* in 1800 when he said, "The entrepreneur shifts economic resources out of an area of lower and into an area of higher productivity and greater yield." The article describes entrepreneurship as the special collection of skills possessed by an entrepreneur. These skills include a propensity to take risks over and above the normal in an effort to create wealth. Entrepreneurs are people who find ways around business difficulties; they persevere with a business plan at times when others run for the shelter of full-time employment elsewhere. The article further goes on to describe an entrepreneur as "somebody who offers an innovative solution to problems and creation of ventures."

This article gives the sense that an entrepreneur acts independently. The paradox is, many entrepreneurs do not act independently. The seemingly individualized activities of entrepreneurs can sometimes thrive through cooperation and interdependence. Given our present understanding of how entrepreneurs develop and operate, entrepreneurship is often a team activity, rather than the sole responsibility of an individual entrepreneur. Although the entrepreneur may play the role of leader, the social dynamics enveloping the entrepreneur are also likely to be significant in bringing entrepreneurship to life.

In 1986, Gifford Pinchot III, an American entrepreneur, author and inventor, coined the term *intrapreneur*, which he defined as the entrepreneurial individual who interacts within their paid work environment discovering, evaluating, and exploiting opportunities.

The term *intrapreneur* is defined by the American Heritage Dictionary as "a person within a corporation who takes direct responsibility for turning an idea into a profitable finished product through assertive risk-taking and innovation." In 1988, Stanford

University Business Professor Robert Burgleman adopted the term *intrapreneur* in his seminal work, *"Managing the Internal Corporate Venturing Process,"* to describe an entrepreneurial individual who interacts within their paid work environment—discovering, evaluating, exploiting opportunities, and influencing the creation of new corporate resources.

In part because of the lack of clarity around the concepts, entrepreneur, and entrepreneurship, intrapreneur and intrapreneurship have become all-encompassing words with associated misconceptions. For example, in a special report that appeared in the March 14th, 2009, edition of *The Economist*, it was boldly stated that most people erroneously view the word *entrepreneur* as referring to anyone who starts a business—large or small, yet business entry and innovation are fundamentally different activities than managing a business. Not everyone that starts a business is an entrepreneur. Business people, like entrepreneurs, are found wearing many hats and their normal functions are a mix of operations, management, promotion, and leadership activities.

There is also confusion around the term "intrapreneurship." Although most entrepreneurs work independently, many do not. The entrepreneurs who work independently operate with limited contact or cooperation with others and do not seek intricate interdependencies. However, it is a paradox that the seemingly individualized activities of entrepreneurs can sometimes thrive through cooperation and interdependence. Individual entrepreneurs have often joined forces via informal networks and contacts to gain information, assistance, and start-up capital.

Business incubators, clusters, intrapreneurship, and hive systems are all forms of collaborative team entrepreneurship.

These are all emerging models for communities or groups that choose to start or reinvent business development from the inside out. This is of particular relevance to entrepreneurship education in Canada where expanding First Nations populations and growth in Asian and African immigrant populations are headline news. In 2000, 85% of people entering the job market for the first time were women and minorities. Many youth, women, immigrants, and Indigenous people seek approaches in social structure, business, and education that are sensitive to their experiences and attuned to identifying and responding to the range of developmental needs that they present.

The intrapreneur is described as an employee transforming ideas either into new or improved products or services within an existing organization. The terms *intrapreneur* and *intrapreneurship* pepper discussions from scholars to business leaders to the extent that the concept may lead people to presume an emergence of a new social, scientific, or economic phenomenon. Robert M. Adams, General Manager of 3M's New Business Ventures Division declares that he had intrapreneurs for years at 3M but didn't know what to call them. The term seems new today because from time-to-time new terms or expressions for old situations rise to common usage in our everyday vocabulary.

However, uncertainty and ambiguity continue to surround entrepreneurial activities generated through forms of collaboration, cooperation, and interdependence. A list of specific traits and behaviours for those who choose to work in this manner remains elusive and ill defined. As with independent entrepreneurs, intrapreneurs learn from their failures and successes, use this experience in their next enterprise activity, and process information in an intuitive way.

On this larger business front, for example, 3M, Pfizer, Virgin, Campbell's, Microsoft, IBM, and Hewlett Packard, are concerned about losing both market share and entrepreneurial talent to an ever-increasing percentage of independent start-ups. Companies and organizations and overall economies are mindful of the need to speed up the process of inventing and commercializing innovative products and services and to keep pace with technology. Competitiveness in all spheres is renewed through loosely connected independent ventures—the ones that generate and exploit new technologies, products, or businesses.

Many organizations have resolved to bring entrepreneurial thinking inside the organization in the form of intrapreneurship to act as a centerpiece in organizational efforts to solve the need for constant innovation. By enhancing risk taking and proactive responses to environmental changes, these enterprises encourage the entrepreneurial behaviours that characterize the impetus of original business creation. Intrapreneurship is no longer left to either chance or serendipity. Companies have incorporated networking between sections as a way to infuse the learning, creativity, and innovation deemed as essential within corporate entrepreneurship.

Additionally, management of the core enterprise developed a variety of business support resources and services, to accelerate the successful development of internal entrepreneurship. Several career options now exist related to entrepreneurship within organizations; the internal promotion of entrepreneurship skills has led to career paths as an intrapreneur, management change agent, and entrepreneurial executive to facilitate the process and deploy resources.

Whether working within a corporation or acting alone, entrepreneurs, in all manifestations, are involved in a creative process—not simply the generation of a great idea that requires funding to start and management skills to operate along a linear path.

The implication of these above concepts shifts the entre-preneurship education emphasis away from lone business start-up and ownership and highlights a range of associated careers and professions that contribute to and are intrinsically linked to the economic outcomes associated with the phenomenon of entrepreneurship.

Chapter 2

Entrepreneurship as an Economic Driver

The 1980s were years of increasing international competition and rapid technological change. The global workplace became dramatically flexible with the arrival of the Internet, cellular phones, and personal computers. The rapid expansion of electronic commerce facilitated entrepreneurial activity across borders. Economic changes such as downsizing by larger companies and the outsourcing of labour to overseas markets brought with them recognition that both entrepreneurship and small business were key to creating employment innovation, improving competitiveness, and encouraging economic development.

In his 1985 book, *Innovation and Entrepreneurship,* management thought leader Peter Drucker alerted business managers and education administrators to the emergence of the entrepreneurial economy, in which he said entrepreneurship would play a crucial role in a country's economic growth. He further stated that there would be strong connections between entrepreneurship, the diffusion of new technologies, and a country's international competitiveness. Drucker compared the emergence of the entrepreneurial economy of today with that of the industrial capitalist economy. Both are based on innovation and on the creation and exploitation of invention.

Today, companies are increasingly mindful of the need to speed up the process of inventing and commercializing innovative products and services and to keep pace with technology. This will require a proactive attitude and a focus on entrepreneurship.

As Indiana University professor David Audretsch noted in a 2002 study, people often believe a company's and country's international competitiveness will be renewed through loosely connected independent ventures that generate and exploit new technologies, products, or businesses. As Montpellier Business School Professor Roy Thurik and Maastrict University Professor Martin Caree stressed in a 2010 study, it is not that simple. Entrepreneurship plays a central role in creating new companies, new jobs and new ideas to add significant value to organizations, countries, and the global economy. There must be a proactive attitude toward innovation and the creation of new ventures, otherwise companies will be unlikely to survive in an increasingly aggressive, competitive, and dynamic marketplace.

Despite the general agreement on the importance of entrepreneurship, there exists a diversity of thinking about entrepreneurship as a phenomenon and lack of agreement in the framing of entrepreneurship, both conceptually and in practice. According to Australian researchers Yamin and O'Connor, the relationship between entrepreneurship and the broad concept of business is often blurred as well. These researchers noted this blurring is due to many writers on the topic of entrepreneurship using the differentiation method of 1930s Austrian economist Joseph Schumpeter. He drew a division between the activities of an enterprise (an organization that is responsible for economic development through innovation and the creation of new markets and new market dynamics) and the activities of a business (an organization that is responsible for economic growth and the efficient production and distribution of goods and services for existing market dynamics).

Thousands of small firms have been founded. in recent years, established by women, minorities, and immigrants; as a result, small firms have made a formidable contribution to economies. Due to the number of firms who hired one or two employees, during the decade of the 1990s, more than 1 million net new jobs were created in North America alone. According to Australian researcher Per Davidsson, the view is that the entrepreneurship phenomenon is a micro-level behaviour that has "hugely important macro-level implications." The economic and social contributions of entrepreneurs, new companies, and family businesses have been shown to make immensely disproportionate contributions to job creation, innovation, and economic renewal, compared with the contributions that the 500 or so largest companies make.

Large organizations concerned about losing both market share and are mindful of the need to speed up the process of inventing and commercializing innovative products and services

If companies and organizations do not adopt a proactive attitude toward innovation and the creation of new ventures,

they are unlikely to survive in an increasingly aggressive, competitive, and dynamic marketplace.

Chapter 3

Entrepreneurship Education – A Focus on the Individual, the Process, or the Organization?

Given the critical importance of entrepreneurship, it is vital that it be embraced by the educational system.

At essence is the entrepreneur's ability to envision and chart a course for a venture by combining a way of thinking to bridge innovative discoveries and operational techniques, all in the context of extraordinary uncertainty and ambiguity. Entrepreneurs in all manifestations are involved in a creative process to generate innovative action.

Since the early 1980s, governments and international organizations such as the European Foundation for Management Development have steered research into the development of an entrepreneurship culture and are actively encouraging the education sector to marshal their resources and expertise to stimulate entrepreneurship teaching and small business creation.

They have sought to nurture enterprise culture and have openly espoused the proposition that entrepreneurial qualities can be developed through the education system. Governments are also seeking to employ entrepreneurship education as a means to stimulate increased levels of economic activity. As Professor Paul Hannon at the UK-based National Centre for Entrepreneurship observes, entrepreneurship development is now central to many government policies. Strathclyde University Professor Alicia Coduras Martínez supports Hannon's position, noting that policymakers frequently consider the possibility of entrepreneurship education and training as an "efficient mechanism for increasing entrepreneurial activity."

In their 2011 work, Heidi Neck and Patricia Greene of Babson College describe the various types of entrepreneurship education sought through the lens of each of three primary worldviews. These worldviews are: the entrepreneurial individual, the entrepreneurial process and entrepreneurial cognition.

The entrepreneurial individual worldview of education treats the entrepreneur as a hero figure. This places emphasis on the entrepreneur, the entrepreneurial team, and the thinking and decision making that underpins successful entrepreneur outcomes. This human attribute concept has tended to manifest as enterprise education that generally has a preoccupation with developing the enterprising actor. From this perspective, entrepreneurship education tends to take the form of contrasting the student with ideal types of entrepreneurs and prompting behaviours from students to cast themselves in the mold of entrepreneur role models.

The entrepreneurial process worldview adopts an analytical approach and moves away from attempting to embed specific entrepreneurial traits. In this form of education, the organization becomes a focal point and curricula favours the processes of opportunity recognition and evaluation, new venture formation, and business planning. The pedagogical model assumes that by undertaking specific process tasks, entrepreneurial outcomes become more predictable. Students are being prepared for entrepreneurship by learning the processes they should replicate.

The entrepreneurial cognition worldview focuses on competitive marketplaces, strategic positioning and incremental innovation as a means to reposition, redeploy, and develop new resources and capabilities.

It is important to understand these distinctions in worldviews. None of the three attempts to narrowly define entrepreneurship to fit into any one economic framework. This is a good thing. The implication is that entrepreneurship education should include elements of different world views and different degrees of practice and theory depending on the specific education content.

Chapter 4

Can Entrepreneurship Be Taught?

Debate amongst academic researchers centers around the extent to which entrepreneurship can be taught. East Anglia Polytechnic academics Kazam Chaharbaghi and Robert Willis maintain that entrepreneurs cannot be manufactured, only recognized. This view supports a common belief that entrepreneurs are born not made. Ian Deamer and Louise Earle of Plymouth University along with Allan Gibb of Durham University maintain that some people have been born with exceptional personalities that impel them towards innovative and highly creative commercial behaviour.

Henry Etkopwitz of the International Triple Helix Institute argues that entrepreneurship is a learned competency rather than an inherited predisposition or cultural trait. As Mercy Anselm of

York University suggests individuals may be born with propensities toward entrepreneurship, but the level of entrepreneurship activity will be higher if entrepreneurial skills are taught.

After years of back-and-forth argument, business educators have now evolved beyond the myth that entrepreneurs are born, not made. Management thinker Peter Drucker said that there is nothing magical about the entrepreneurial mystique; that it is not mysterious, and it has nothing to do with the genes. It is a discipline, and like any discipline, it can be learned. Additional support for this view comes from Memorial University academics Gary Gorman, Dennis Hanlon and Wayne King and their 10-year literature review of enterprise, entrepreneurship, and small business management education that reported, "Most of the empirical studies surveyed indicated that entrepreneurship can be taught, or at least encouraged, by entrepreneurship education."

In 2003, Professor Lowell Busenitz (University of Oklahoma) and colleagues examined 97 entrepreneurship articles published in leading management journals from 1985 to 1999. The goal was to provide evidence of the emergence of entrepreneurship as an academic field. Their study found evidence that entrepreneurship is emerging but had not yet arrived. They found that no research "space" in entrepreneurship had yet been defined, leaving the field permeable to other disciplines. They noted that until intellectual boundaries are established, the field may never gain the consensus and legitimacy academics seek and may only be viewed as a venue in which other disciplinary perspectives may be tested.

In 2003, Jerome Katz at St. Louis University presented the argument that if entrepreneurship education is to grow, the lack of faculty is the number one limiting factor that must be dealt with.

Closely behind this first limiting factor is the lack of PhD programs creating faculty to teach entrepreneurship studies.

In 2004, researchers at George Washington University developed a survey to examine the current state of entrepreneurial education in the United States and internationally and to evaluate the extent and breadth of entrepreneurial education methods and course offerings during the 2004-2005 academic year. The survey indicated that the trends discovered in previous surveys conducted from 1977-2000 had continued on a similar path. Survey results showed the traditional teaching method of requiring students to create business plans still exists as a foundation for teaching the nuts and bolts of entrepreneurship and small business management.

Yet, the data also showed that educational institutions are moving towards a more knowledge sharing ecology where class discussions and guest speakers are becoming more popular. The use of periodicals and magazines such as *The Wall Street Journal*, *Entrepreneur Magazine*, and *Business Week* has continued to supplement the information base for both entrepreneurship educators and students alike, allowing both educators and students to apply the theories presented in class with real life examples that reflect the pulse of the market.

Chapter 5

The Effectiveness of Entrepreneurship Education

Since 2003-2004, major strides have been made worldwide in the area of entrepreneurship education. As of 2013, Bruce Martin, Jeffrey McNally, and Michael Kay of Thomson Rivers University, University of New Brunswick and Wilfred Laurier University respectively identified at least 19 studies investigating the effectiveness of entrepreneurship courses and programs across 14 countries.

What remains is for entrepreneurship education to develop further conceptual and theoretical aspects. To achieve this, Wang, Wong, and Lu of the National University of Singapore suggest a complex three-stage model to take into account : key demographic, educational, motivational attitude, perceived interest, and feasibility factors. This multi-faceted approach is required because a tendency or inclination toward entrepreneurship cannot be isolated to a solitary cause. Studies have revealed coupled or multiple links between entrepreneurship, education, and individual personality characteristics as German researchers Christian Lüthje and Nikolaus Franke remind us.

Current literature explains that the entrepreneurial learning style prefers active experimentation, with some balance between concrete experience and abstract conceptualization. Entrepreneurs appear to learn primarily through doing and reflection, which includes acquiring information through copying and from opportunities that emerge from making mistakes.

Preliminary research in 2004 by University of Johannesburg researchers Cecile Nieuwenhuizen and Darelle Groenwald on the brain preference profiles of entrepreneurs appears to confirm the right-brain thinking preferences of successful entrepreneurs. The left-brain requires hard facts before reaching a decision, specializes in precise descriptions and exact explanations, and demands structure and certainty, while the right-brain is happier dealing with uncertainties and elusive knowledge, enjoys analogies, simile, and metaphors, and thrives on spontaneity and ambiguity. Those with right-brain thinking favour open-ended questions and problems for which there are many answers, rather than a single correct solution.

However, thinking creatively, or colloquially out of the box, is a necessary but not wholly sufficient criterion for defining the entrepreneur. Divergent or creative thinking must be within an appropriate context that is aligned with true entrepreneurial behaviour. **It is not possible to proceed in absolute terms— to assume convergent thinkers are not creative, divergent thinkers are creative, or that the highly creative child will be entrepreneurial.**

Chapter 6

The Influence of Government and NGOs on Entrepreneurial Education

In its 2011 report on skills for innovation and research, the Organization for Economic Co-operation and Development (OECD) suggests that a broad range of abilities is an increasingly important contributor to innovation in a nation. This report also argues that entrepreneurial skills and capabilities are an essential element for an innovation system.

Entrepreneurship development is now central to many government policies. The Australian government policy states: *to influence economic growth, policymakers should support and encourage the provision of entrepreneurship education to connect new ideas, technologies and new applications of knowledge to business formation and expansion.*

The Norwegian national strategic plan for entrepreneurship development within the education system led to the creative K–12 innovation camps (with special attention to young women) in which pupils in youth enterprises may participate (Government of Norway, 2010). The Junior Achievement Young Enterprise (JA-YE) Norway is organized as a non-governmental organization (NGO) and is a private provider of entrepreneurship education in Norway. JA-YE Norway's activities have expanded greatly since the organization was established in 1997, and JA-YE Norway now offers programs for all levels of education and training from Kindergarten through to higher education. JA-YE Norway is part of an extensive international collaboration network.

Members of JA-YE Europe comprise a broad collaboration between 40 countries, based on the same learning platform. This NGO provides opportunities for young people to experience and understand the significance of contact across borders. JA-YE Norway lists the following five criteria for identifying and quality assuring programs promoting pupils' and students' entrepreneurial competence: (a) they are to promote creative processes; (b) they are to be based on active learning on the part of the pupils; (c) they must be cross disciplinary; (d) they must strengthen collaboration between the school and the local community; and (e) they must focus on promoting financial, social, or cultural wealth creation.

In the United States, organizations like the Indianapolis Mind Trust have sponsored Education Entrepreneur Fellowships. This initiative has attracted over 1,300 people from 48 states and 31 countries who share their innovative teaching approaches in entrepreneurship education. Another organization, the Consortium of Entrepreneurship Education has been providing leadership and gathering enthusiasm for teaching entrepreneurship since 1982.

Its mission is to: *champion entrepreneurship education, cultivating students for a prosperous future. Through leadership, professional development, advocacy, and networking, EntreEd is the curator of educational practices and programs that forge entrepreneurial capabilities in all students.* The consortium was formed in response to the groundswell of requests that entrepreneurship should be part of the curriculum of all vocational programs. This growing collection of scholars in the field of entrepreneurship have developed a mission to identify leading-edge research issues and domains and develop high profile research initiatives that demonstrate the highest level of scholarship to entrepreneurship centres and the academic community at large. The consortium has become the focal point for entrepreneurship centres across the United States to continue the advancement of entrepreneurial excellence.

In 2000, the National Consortium of Entrepreneurship Centers was founded for the purpose of continued collaboration among the established entrepreneurship centres, as well as the newer emerging centres, to work together to share information, develop special projects, and assist each other in advancing and improving their centres' impact.

Chapter 7

Entrepreneurship as a K-12 Curriculum

A 2009 Ernst & Young study estimated that as many as 5.6 million Americans younger than age 34 were actively trying to start their own business; one third of new entrepreneurs are younger than age 30; more than 60% of people 18–29 years of age say they want to own their own businesses; and nearly 80% of would-be entrepreneurs in the United States are between the ages of 18 and 34. With these explosive numbers, it is no wonder that entrepreneurial education in North America continues to be on the rise.

Enterprise education is commonly interpreted to mean developing entrepreneurs; however, the K-12 system in North America has taken the approach that not all entrepreneurship students need to be, or could be, an entrepreneur. Many students and others just wish to be educated about all manifestations of the entrepreneur, entrepreneurial careers, and entrepreneurship, including what it is, how it works, and its contribution to society.

From a simple view, this means that K–12 entrepreneurship classes should educate "for," "through," and "about" enterprise. This approach diverts attention away from any specific economic interests or outcomes towards the development of entrepreneurial thinking. Along with the benefits to economies, entrepreneurial thinking can be applied by students to any situation in life that requires the navigation and negotiation of unpredictability; the need for ingenuity and innovation in problem solving, creativity, flexibility, self-direction, and the ability to respond to widely different situations.

A core objective of entrepreneurship education should be to differentiate it from typical business education, as business entry is a fundamentally different activity than managing a business.

To achieve an effective blend of science and art, Allan Gibb of Durham University suggested in 2002 a multidisciplinary approach in entrepreneurship education with teaching that involves both the sciences (business and management competencies) and the arts (creative and innovative thinking). James Fiet of Louisville University stated that student-led activities in the classroom should be combined with teaching of underlying theories.

The question then becomes, what should be taught? As early as 2004, Donald Kuratko of Indiana University argued that the content required in entrepreneurship education is threefold (1) the knowledge component (or the science of entrepreneurship), (2) the innovation and creativity that satisfy the need for entrepreneurial novelty, and (3) the navigation of uncertainty (or the *art* of entrepreneurship).

Chapter 8

Entrepreneurial Teaching – The Science and the Art

The knowledge component was addressed in a 2000 paper by David Rae of De Montfort University who pointed out that K–12 entrepreneurship education typically tackles the science of entrepreneurship by providing a conceptual background and stimulating analytical thought processes of business and functional management competencies. Teachers ensure K–12 students are made aware of entrepreneur career options, sources of venture capital, idea protection, ambiguity tolerance, the characteristics that define the entrepreneurial personality, and the challenges associated with each stage of venture development.

Through instruction, students learn to speak the language of business on such matters as how to raise finance, the selection of premises, taxation, elementary bookkeeping, employment, and legal regulations. Rae further points out how through entrepreneurship curricula, such as the Province of Saskatchewan's *Entrepreneurship 30* course offered at the 9–12 grade levels, students examine the entrepreneurial process in which the entrepreneur generates ideas, recognizes opportunities, determines the feasibility of ideas, markets, plans the venture, and identifies needed resources using a business plan.

Students are exposed to knowledge, resources, and experiences to prepare for entrepreneurial career paths and managerial skills required to cope with the myriad of expectations and demands faced when starting new ventures, including identification of opportunities in the marketplace, and the knowledge and skills necessary to capitalize and manage these opportunities. Marketing and challenges such as cash flow are addressed from the small business owner's point of view. Enterprise development, including skill-building courses in negotiation, leadership, new product development, and exposure to technological innovation, helps students to act in an entrepreneurial manner.

The creativity component is more elusive. Entrepreneurship, in all its manifestations, is a creative process, not simply the generation of a great idea that requires funding to start and management skills to operate along a linear path. As early as 1999, Lancaster University researchers Sarah Jack and Alistair Anderson argued that entrepreneurship programs in the K–12 system should provide students with a rich understanding of the entrepreneurial process and enable them to be ready to react to circumstances not yet known or entirely predictable. They further said programs should contain a dimension that is inductive, subjective, and involves "perceptual leaps which may transcend a conventional economic rationality." The underpinning theme is that an entrepreneur must possess is creativity to generate enterprise, understand innovation, and satisfy the search for entrepreneurial novelty and navigation of uncertainty.

Chapter 9

Current State of K-12 Entrepreneurship Education

Some still question whether many entrepreneurship courses are not simply traditional management courses with a new label. This is not an unfounded claim as some courses are designed to primarily introduce students to the principles of business and tend to teach students how to become proficient employees instead of successful entrepreneurs.

Many K–12 entrepreneurship curricula follow the pattern of predominantly business classes, with the topics of business plan writing, basic accounting, marketing, and recruitment and selection of employees. But entrepreneurship education should not be viewed as some mechanistic or technocratic process but rather as a holistic and integrative process.

In 1997, University of New Mexico researcher John Young found very little uniformity among the programs offered within international education, a broad framework of differences and similarities in perception of the ability to teach entrepreneurial behaviours, and the manner whereby this is best achieved. Three years later, Italian researchers Falkang and Alberti noted it was still apparent that there was little uniformity in content and approach among programs and courses.

In 2000, Rushing and Kent's research on the status of K–12 entrepreneurship education in the United States also concluded that entrepreneurship education was in an embryonic state. Another three years later, Australian researchers, Nicole Peterman and Jessica Kennedy drew attention to the wide variety of entrepreneurship programs on offer in the marketplace and suggested that while positive results may be found from a study of one program, it could not be assumed that all programs would have similar results due to variations in content, pedagogy, and student learning styles.

From 2000 to 2010, there have been at least 20 studies undertaken investigating the effectiveness of entrepreneurship courses and programs across 14 countries. The variety of approaches within K–12 teaching is described and evaluated on an ongoing basis by the highly respected Kauffman-RAND Institute. As well, the Science and Technology Policy Institute regularly conducts its "Survey of Entrepreneurship Education Initiatives" on 26 programs within Finland, Germany, Norway, Spain, and the United Kingdom.

While the science (knowledge component) of entrepreneurial learning is a requirement to enable students to learn "for," "about," "through" entrepreneurship, many students might not wish to become entrepreneurs. This teaching focus, then, contrasts sharply with the reality of the entrepreneur who will be operating with intuition and limited information under acute time pressure.

Instead of just the knowledge component, what is needed is experiential learning. Students must be given a chance to enhance their individual capacity for innovative behaviour, creativity, flexibility, self-direction, and the ability to respond to widely different situations.

An Overview of the Problem in K-12

The literature indicates entrepreneurship is important in our society, entrepreneurship teaching is meaningful, and that experiential learning is a viable approach to teaching entrepreneurship. But teacher training remains an issue.

K–12 classroom efforts focus on the science of entrepreneurship and are dominated by finding one great idea and the development of a business plan produced in a lock-step pattern. This is a continuance of the old-school teaching approach that conveys knowledge to learners through a conventional lecture format using a top-down transmission methodology. This approach ignores the *art* of the entrepreneurial thinking process—it may even inhibit the development of the requisite entrepreneurial attitudes and skills.

When experiential learning is present in the K-12 system, the predominant teaching approach "through" the subject is a one-off mock-up venture, not a process of innovative thinking to exploit opportunities that promote long-lasting entrepreneurial behaviour, nor are students presented with starting new ventures inside established organizations (intrapreneurship) that prepare them and their employers for entrepreneurial thinking in this rapidly changing world.

Very few teachers have received any training or development in the field of entrepreneurship education. Teachers who possess backgrounds in such fields as marketing, organizational behaviour, personnel management, logistics, social psychology, or accounting and finance find themselves "volunteered" to teach entrepreneurship. Some teachers remain largely unaware of the trends in business (such as intrapreneurship) and there are few textbooks written that include information on the principles of invention, innovation, and entrepreneurship.

Dr. Jeff Cornwall, the Jack C. Massey Chair in Entrepreneurship at Belmont University, wrote that very few teachers have received any training or development in the field of entrepreneurship education. British researchers McKeown, Millman, Sursani, Smith, and Martin noted that the majority of entrepreneurship educators surveyed claim they offer practical entrepreneurship courses (57%). A very small proportion offer theoretical courses (5%), and 25% claimed to offer a mix of theory and practice. The reality was that only a very small number (3%) made use of action and experiential learning approaches, which are regarded as the most effective methods for educating entrepreneurs.

Luke Pittaway of Ohio University added support to the argument in 2007 with a survey that showed 43% of entrepreneurship educators were using multiple methods for content delivery, but only based on traditional techniques such as lectures, workshops, and seminars.

As British researchers Adcroft, Willis, and Dhaliwal stressed in 2004, entrepreneurship education that restricts itself to management skills can contribute somewhat to the provision of technical skills of entrepreneurs (learning "for" and "about" entrepreneurship), but it cannot contribute to the element of serendipity, particularly the learning "through" that is central to entrepreneurship.

Given the current state of entrepreneurship education, the evolving demands of the marketplace and our present understanding of how entrepreneurs develop and operate, there is a gap in our knowledge and understanding on how experiential learning can affect teachers' instructional approaches to introduce the *art* of entrepreneurship in its many manifestations.

And it was this above problem that drove me to do my research for my PhD. The purpose of my PhD research was to study and understand the lived experiences of a group of teachers who were introducing experiential learning into the Saskatchewan education system via Entrepreneurship 30 classes. My aim was to represent the discovery, insight, understanding and skill that participants in this research had when they rejected, adopted, or adapted the experiential learning exercises to which they had been introduced.

The questions in my research originated from my curiosity to discover if there is a case for incorporating a set of experiential exercises related to the *art* of entrepreneurial thinking and the concept of intrapreneurship into the current curricula?

Furthermore, I wanted to discover: when the research participants were exposed to and trained in the use of experiential learning to explain manifestations of entrepreneurship, including intrapreneurship, how would they incorporate the exercise in their teaching, what effects would they observe in the participation and work of their students—and finally, what was the interest in intrapreneurship?

Chapter 10

Teaching Entrepreneurial Thinking Through Experiential Exercises

In *Entrepreneurship in Small and Medium Sized Enterprises and the Macro Economy*, University of Reading Professor Mark Casson writes that the hallmarks of entrepreneurs are creativity and learning through trial and error—not adherence to the tenets of business formulae.

Whether students are learning "for," "about," or "through" entrepreneurship, the focus needs to shift from the traditional to placing emphasis on learning by doing and providing opportunities for students to actively participate in as well as control and mold the learning situation. In short, entrepreneurial programs should be geared toward creativity, multidisciplinary and process-orientated approaches, and theory-based practical applications experienced in the classroom setting. Rather than a focus on systems and techniques, entrepreneurial education should inculcate the necessary attitudes, values, and psychological sets and develop appropriate personal attributes such as innovativeness, the willingness to take risks and to fail and start afresh, creativity determination, and self-direction.

If the practice of entrepreneurship education is one that requires a blend of knowledge, skills, and attitudes, then there is a need for a shift to learning in an environment with as genuine entrepreneurship experiences as possible. Students need to develop solutions under pressure, glean information from a range of sources, and learn from failure. This active approach requires teachers as facilitators, not the controllers of the learning of students. This requires the tolerance of experimentation by the teachers and the active encouragement of errors. They must follow the premise that the entrepreneurial learning style prefers active experimentation with some balance between concrete experience and abstract conceptualization. The best methods suited to this entrepreneurial learning style are active-applied and active-experimentation, including concrete experience, reflective observation, and abstract conceptualization. Students examine the process needed to understand innovation and creativity to satisfy the search for entrepreneurial novelty and navigation of uncertainty. This active approach can be summed up by the descriptor "experiential learning."

In 2002, Scottish researchers Laura Galloway and Wendy Brown wrote: "If we apply the concept of experiential learning to the field of entrepreneurship, it implies that the method will ensure that the students will learn the relevant theories but will also enable them to master an area of knowledge which they otherwise barely would recognize."

Experiential Learning

Experiential learning speaks to learning by doing. This is not a new concept. In 340 B.C., Aristotle wrote, "For the things we have to learn before we can do them, we learn by doing them."

In the early 1900s, John Dewey, an American educational theorist, likened education to living, as a process of experiencing. He believed that students must interact with their environment in order to adapt and learn. Dewey felt the same idea was true for teachers and that teachers and students must learn together.

In his experiential learning theory, former Case Western Reserve Professor David A. Kolb proposed as early as 1994 that people experience real situations, to observe and reflect on these, form or modify concepts and theories, and seek to test these in a new situation. He wrote, "Learning is the process whereby knowledge is created through the transformation of experience." He said this happens by learners engaging intellectually, emotionally, socially, and/or physically. Relationships are developed and nurtured learner to self, learner to others, and learner to the world at large. This involvement helps produce a perception that the learning task is authentic. Individuals may experience success, failure, risk-taking, and uncertainty, as the outcomes of experience cannot be fully predicted. The results of the learning are personal and form the basis for future experiences and learning.

In 1997, University of Northern Colorado researcher John Luckner and colleague Reldan Nadler explained Kolb's theory of how this happens through experiential exercises. The learner is a participant, rather than a spectator in the experiential learning process, and is actively engaged in posing questions, investigating, experimenting, being curious, solving problems, assuming responsibility, being creative, and constructing meaning.

Writing in 2003, University of Calgary researcher Susann Laverty said, "Consciousness is not separate from the world ... but is a formation of historically lived experience.... Understanding is a basic form of human existence in that understanding is not a way we know the world, but rather the way we are.... Historically, a person's history or background, includes what a culture gives a person from birth and is handed down, presenting ways of understanding the world. Through this understanding, one determines what is "real", yet ... one's background cannot be made completely explicit.... People and the world [are] indissolubly related in cultural, in social and in historical contexts."

In 2004, Luke Pittaway of Ohio University said that experiential learning occurs when meaning is made from a direct experience. He explained that this learning has three components:

- knowledge - based on concepts, facts, information, and prior experience;
- activity - based on knowledge applied to current ongoing activities; and
- reflection - based on analysis and assessment of one's own activities.

In this manner, experiential learning is a proactive, problem-solving, and flexible approach that requires an increased focus on reality and experientially based pedagogies.

In the Vlerick Leuven Gent University working paper series 2010/11, researcher Eva Cools describes how a combination series of pre-test, post-test, self-perceived change measurements of entrepreneurial intent, creativity, and attitudes towards entrepreneurs and entrepreneurship were utilized to test 21 programs among 3,130 students. **The researchers found that the higher the intensity of experiential learning within the entrepreneurship program, the stronger the impact on the perceived feasibility of entrepreneurship as a career, perceived desirability, and propensity to act in an enterprising manner.**

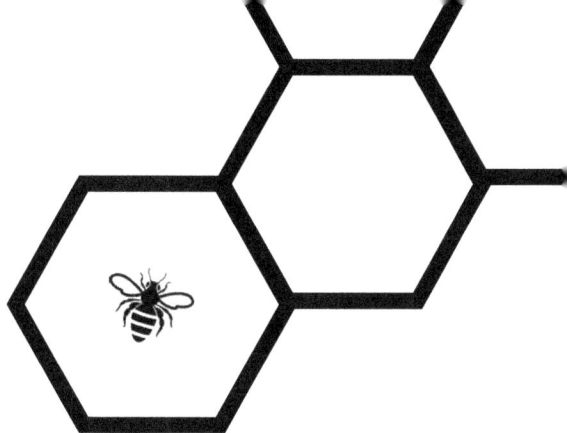

Chapter 11

Taking Intrapreneurship to the Classroom

My Ph.D. research study was an in-depth investigation of a single group of participant teachers, informed by participants, theoretical considerations, and my own personal interaction as the researcher. Over a ten-year period prior to my doctoral studies, I amassed anecdotal evidence that led me to believe that my teaching approach with experiential exercises stimulated entrepreneurial thinking and the *art* of entrepreneurship for the women involved with my own start-up business ventures. I also had anecdotal evidence from my role as a guest teacher in Saskatchewan Learning Entrepreneurship 30 classes where I encouraged students, through experiential exercises, to be creative, muck around, copy from each other, experiment through trial and error—and work as part of a team yet remain apart from the group.

My Ph.D. research, coupled with my own experience about how entrepreneurs and students learn the *art* of entrepreneurial thinking, led me to decode my exercises into a written format that met the rigour of academia, incorporated the principles of experiential learning, and simulate the complexities of the environments in which some entrepreneurs as employees actually operate.

I designed these experiential exercises to encourage students to

- ask if there are other ways of doing things
- challenge custom, routine, and tradition
- be reflective
- critically engage an issue from a variety of perspectives
- realize that there may be more than one right answer
- see mistakes and failures as pit stops on the route to success
- relate seemingly unrelated ideas to generate a solution; and
- see an issue from a broader perspective and, at the same time, to focus on an area in need of change

I then crafted an instruction manual incorporating the set of exercises and props for teachers to include, exclude, or adapt to suit their own teaching artistry.

To accompany the exercises, there are lesson plans and descriptions of teaching techniques that require teachers to facilitate, not control, the learning process. The manual explains how the exercise process encourages student abilities to be activated and experienced in a creative manner, rather than by the teacher instructing, proffering knowledge, or presenting or offering personal wisdom as absolute.

With research participants, I worked through the experiential exercises. I considered that my role was also to nurture participants to the point at which they understood the exercises and expressed confidence to make logistical decisions within their current teaching of Entrepreneurship to introduce, adapt, or discard the experiential exercises. The concepts of entrepreneurial thinking were then understood by the participants and any misconceptions that entrepreneurship is always a one-track venture by an individual or group are overcome. I emphasized that intrapreneurship is barely covered (two pages) in the current curriculum, and the explanation understates the impact of the phenomenon in current business trends.

I shared the purpose and objectives of the research and gave background on the *art* and *science* of entrepreneurship and collaborative individualism within entrepreneurship (intrapreneurship). With the experiential exercises, the teachers became, not the controllers of learning, but facilitators in order that students experience the *art* of entrepreneurial thinking and the process for themselves.

After the workshop, I provided each participant with a manual of the exercises and the resources required to conduct each exercise. I then followed their progress for a period of six weeks to determine if, how, and why they implemented the experiential activities into their teaching.

Throughout the two-day workshop and our later conversations, several findings came to light:

1. The training helped the teachers to be more confident in teaching entrepreneurship in the experiential way. Having the exercises and the training to lead them built confidence in being able to teach entrepreneurship even when one had not been an entrepreneur or had not facilitated previously. One participant said, *"The exercises have eliminated any anxiety I felt about lack of control in the classroom."* It was important that individuals new to experiential learning can experience for themselves and have the opportunity for discussion. After the completion of the full set of exercises, the research participants concluded that the exercises had unveiled manifestations of the entrepreneurship process and the "art" of entrepreneurial thinking for themselves.

2. Teachers, administrators, students and parents are not always clear on the purpose of facilitation versus direct teaching, the value of facilitation, the differences between facilitation and direct teaching, and the reasons for using each modality at different times.

3. Teachers sometimes struggle with moving away from a didactic teaching style, seeing time using a facilitation style as *"taking away from teaching time"* and using experiential exercises as *"playing games."* The teacher's role in facilitation is not taking the conversational lead in the classroom, but rather by stepping back and allowing students to experience learning through trial and error. Some teachers are reluctant to step away from direct teaching and will not like to teach by way of facilitation because of discomfort or a perceived loss of control.

4. There is a skepticism with the rationale for learning through failure versus being shown best practice—learning by doing instead of learning by being told. (I shared with the group that I sometimes encounter teachers and others who step in to "help me" answer questions raised by students. As I continuously redirect students to discuss all the questions they raise in their groups, I sometimes feel that other teachers think I do not know the answers or that that the role of teachers is to answer all the questions.)

5. The concept of intrapreneurship was in direct odds with popular media promoting the individual entrepreneur; determining success based on a money-making business versus successfully developing entrepreneurship skills. A student can get A+ on a competition but fail at developing entrepreneurship skills and mindset. Entrepreneurship competitions are focused on winning the prize and students and schools are rewarded for the best money-making endeavor, not for learning through trial and error. Their success is measuring against the prize instead of the learning. The television show, *The Dragons' Den*, encourages most entrepreneurship students and teachers to believe that the way ahead is to seek funding for one great idea. If you look at the *Dragons' Den*, one of the first questions asked is, "What are your sales?" They don't look at a business that has not yet been successful.

6. Experiential activities might be a particular *"hard sell"* for school administrators who expect direct transmission of

knowledge in a quiet room. Teachers may be perceived to be lazy, letting their students run untamed. The noise level increases with interaction and a teacher may be told to *"tone it down as you are disrupting learning."* It is not just the administrators who think the teacher must be at the front of the room imparting knowledge—this is a perception shared by some students, parents, and colleagues who view any lesson outside the standard approach of transmitting information as being laziness on the part of teachers. The research participants agreed there is a need for (a) a group of recommendations, (b) train-the-trainer sessions, and (c) a link of the exercises to outcomes in order to embed this type of teaching as *"acceptable"* in the current environment of *"traditional teaching"* and that administrators and parents know what is happening and are satisfied that there is learning taking place. *"The research participants suggested that there be proof of the links to justify to students, parents, and administrators that the exercises were not "wasting time" or "taking away from real teaching."*

The training increased the teachers' level of interest and confidence in teaching entrepreneurship as a subject.

I mindfully avoided asking the research participants specific leading questions in regard to the concept of intrapreneurship, such as, "Do you see value in teaching intrapreneurship?" However, their acceptance and enthusiasm over the topic was apparent.

1. The exercises led to an awakening of a broader interest in entrepreneurship for some and an expansion of this knowledge for others. *"Ahas"* were recorded from all

participants, as "through" the experiential exercises, they recognized that intrapreneurship is nothing exotic or revolutionary; it is simply one of a myriad of interpretations of entrepreneurship. It was clear through their expressions of *"aha"* and *"got it"* and their discussion of hives (intrapreneurship), that they relished the insight of this facet of entrepreneurial thinking and fully grasped the concept of intrapreneurship.

2. All participants said at different times that they *"got it,"* and they wished to introduce this manifestation of entrepreneurship and entrepreneurial thinking to their students. From Exercise 1 onwards, several participants immediately begin planning how to incorporate the new learning on intrapreneurship in their classrooms. They described this *"missing link in the curriculum"* and *"intrapreneurship is growth together—where you can be your own boss and work with others."*

3. All participants demonstrated and verbalized that the pre-workshop and exercises had enhanced their knowledge of intrapreneurship and entrepreneurial thinking and renewed their enthusiasm for teaching Entrepreneurship 30 (Saskatchewan Learning, 2004).

4. Two participants felt validated in their promotion of a mixed teaching approach. They gained stature by becoming recognized as "experts" to their colleagues and were willing to mentor others on experiential learning. Another participant moved from referring to the exercises as "yours" to taking ownership of them. A fourth participant gained confidence through the

provision of content on the process of entrepreneurship and by experiencing entrepreneurial thinking "through" the exercises: "I felt until then inside myself that I was not an entrepreneur. Without experiencing it, I didn't know what it looked like! Then I found my drum moving." The most senior of the research participant's lived experience throughout this process was the most transformational. He is now a champion of intrapreneurship and fully understands that "games" need to be facilitated—not instructed.

Barriers to success via my findings and reflections:

As I reflect on the journey of research and the responses and actions of the research participants, I summarize my findings as:

Finding 1: Teachers of entrepreneurship lack entrepreneurial experience.

As teachers of Entrepreneurship 30 (Saskatchewan Learning, 2004), not one of the research participants had entrepreneurial experience. This discovery aligns with the research that very few entrepreneurship teachers have actually received any training or development in the field of entrepreneurship education. The majority of entrepreneurship teachers had moved from conventional business and management teaching and had limited entrepreneurial experience themselves. This is in line with other research findings that teachers possess backgrounds in such fields as marketing, organizational behaviour, personnel management, logistics, social psychology, or accounting and finance, and many have been "volunteered" to teach entrepreneurship. None of the participants in this research had entrepreneurial experience and all had originally been "volunteered" to teach Entrepreneurship 30.

Finding 2: There is a gap between the stated and actual skillset.

When I compared the pre-workshop questionnaire data, which indicated that all participants had a mixed teaching approach, to the actual skills demonstrated in the workshop and beyond, there was a gap between the stated skill of facilitation and participants' actual mastery of the skill. When it came time for the learning to be transferred to students via facilitation, not all the research participants possessed the facilitation or mentoring skills to foster the role change required to suspend or upend a pattern of lecturing—which is required in experiential learning. If these participants did indeed receive instruction in facilitation skills in the past, they had clearly not had the opportunity to practice this skill to attain mastery.

The critical insight during this process was my lack of understanding that teachers may have been *taught* facilitation skills—but not all have *learnt* them—and the significance of this in the research. I believed that facilitation skills were part of the teacher education curriculum and so prior to the research I had not considered pre-testing the participants for this skill. I had erroneously believed that all participants had received facilitation training and mastered the skills required to conduct experiential learning.

I had been trained in facilitation skills as part of my teacher training in Britain and as a training officer in South Africa and therefore my own skill as a facilitator is a natural part of my teaching approach. I am able to facilitate the learning of others through experiential exercises. I witnessed that the level of experience in facilitation skills directly impacted the approach to the exercises and consequently the learning that might be obtained.

Finding 3: The mastery of facilitation is a prerequisite to conduct experiential exercises.

Experiential exercises require the guidance of a teacher with at least a rudimentary competence as a facilitator. The notions of confidence or fear in facilitation, and skill or the lack thereof, emerged repeatedly throughout the participants' lived experiences, demonstrating its critical relevance. It is not a simple matter to provide teachers with exercises and preliminary training and expect them to jump in without the confidence and competence to adopt an experiential approach.

Several participants described experiencing fear, and this fear presented itself as a lack of confidence or a reluctance to conduct the exercises or a fear in losing control. All participants feared that administrators see experiential learning, without specific outcomes, as a waste of time. I find that this was a factor in why participants chose separate routes to implementation. Participants' routes ranged from opting for day-long workshops in order to show the process and allow for the processing of the learning, to using just the first three exercises that the teacher was confident to facilitate, to using segments of the exercises as five-to-ten-minute icebreakers, to following the full sequence of the exercises on five separate "fun days" to avoid the "noise of games" in the regular classroom schedule.

A good teacher of any subject should not only possess a deep knowledge and understanding of the content of their subject (in this instance all manifestations of entrepreneurship and entrepreneurial thinking) but also be a pedagogic expert.

Finding 4: Teachers require resources to implement the exercises.

To effectively incorporate experiential exercises with a facilitation style, even teachers of longstanding tenure may need resources, in-service work, train-the-trainer sessions and mentoring in order to change from the sage-from-the-stage approach to the guided self-discovery that is demanded in these learning scenarios. When teachers are supported as they face new challenges and information, they can learn to do things differently. When some teachers face challenges to independently conduct exercises in an experiential manner, a boost in confidence through training or retraining in facilitation skills and mentoring encourages diving into what, for some teachers, is long forgotten or new white-water territory.

When business teachers are willing to enter this abstract, conceptual, and creative realm, a variety of tools is required. The challenge is even greater when the focus is on teaching corporate entrepreneurship (intrapreneurship) that is rooted in theories of entrepreneurship, while its implementation is usually considered more of a managerial issue.

Finding 5: The exercises do not fit into current scheduling.

Adequate time to teach in this manner as an issue that surfaced throughout the research. Research participants who were experienced facilitators reinforced the notion that time to conduct these exercises is a crucial factor. There is limited meaning for students to make of the exercises if the time allocated in the lesson renders the exercises into segments as icebreakers or push the facilitator to move to didactic teaching.

Appropriate and adequate time is a crucial tool and resource for teachers. The experienced teachers in facilitation, armed with a series of exercises, still require the resource of time to process the learning and inspire the students to think creatively, independently, and critically. While most other disciplines in business fit well into the traditional, synchronous approach to business education, entrepreneurship students do not fit well into a lock-step curriculum that is bound by space and time. It may be that scheduling during flex time classes or setting aside one day to process all the exercises in a workshop may be the preferable way to expand class time and administration support for teaching the *art* processes of entrepreneurial thinking, which requires unique pedagogies and a teacher style that encourage students to progress from being passive attendees in classrooms to being participative in terms of discussion and deriving options for decision making and creativity.

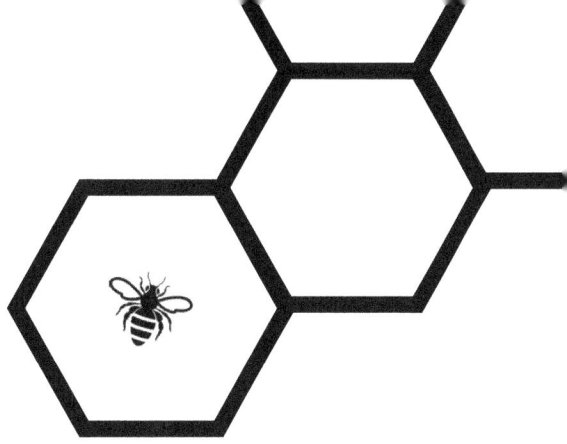

Chapter 12

Conclusion

In the introduction, we discussed the rapid interest in entrepreneurship, for youth, for people in transition, and for women and new Canadians. With these explosive numbers comes a demand for entrepreneurial training beyond the science of entrepreneurship (business courses) to include the art of entrepreneurship (innovation and intrapreneurial thinking). In this book, the case is clearly made that enterprise education should focus beyond only developing entrepreneurs to developing innovative, collaborative thinking as a discipline. It further makes the case that intrapreneurship as a form of entrepreneurship is a powerful approach to launching and maintaining a successful venture.

To that end, the concept of the HIVE was developed.

Most entrepreneurs work independently, many do not. The entrepreneurs who work independently operate with limited contact or cooperation with others and do not seek intricate interdependencies. However, it is a paradox that the seemingly individualized activities of entrepreneurs can sometimes thrive through cooperation and interdependence. In a HIVE system that provides opportunity for teamwork and experimentation, the core business/entrepreneur/queen bee of the hive provides an ongoing learning and economic development framework for fledgling entrepreneurs to simultaneously have an outlet for individual enterprise, their creativity and expression as they launch their own business concept without major financial risk. Often with initially lower outlay and lower financial risks associated, and a support structure that reinforces that failure is education, fledglings are more likely to dream of soaring, and thereby, make tentative steps upward. Participants in the HIVE absorb wisdom and are supported via the income generated from the central proven and viable business of the core entrepreneur.

To develop the skills required for innovative thought that lends itself to intrapreneurship, I developed a series of experiential exercises, six of which are in the following section of this book. **These mimic the six exercises used in my Ph.D. research work which have proven to aid teachers and students in understanding the new concepts involved in the myriad of interpretations of entrepreneurship, including intrapreneurship to "thrive in a hive".**

I continue to offer to co-teach with, mentor, and be mentored by other teachers who wish to follow an experiential learning path. I am constantly discovering like-minded teachers with an experiential approach, who wish

to challenge prevailing notions about entrepreneurship and open new possibilities for everyone, extending the progressive movement in teaching experiential activities in entrepreneurship.

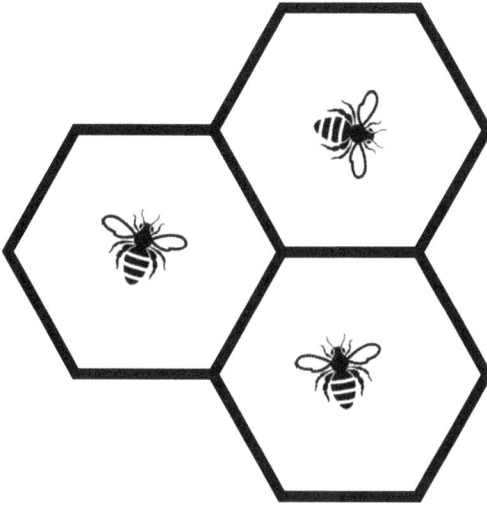

Part Three

Using The Exercises

Supplies for the following six exercises are available in a complete kit through Shosholoza.ca.
(Certain items may be easy for teachers to source locally).

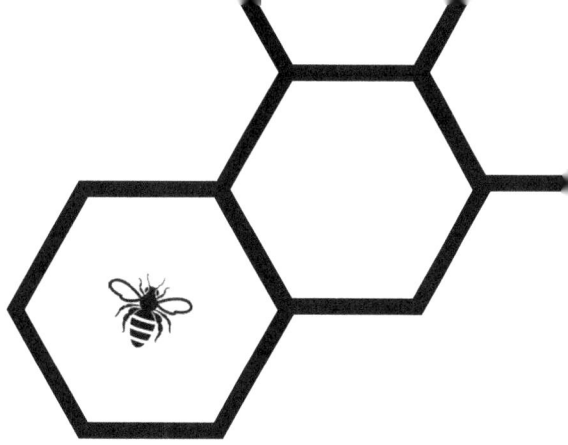

EXERCISE 1

The Art of Entrepreneurial Thinking/ Creativity & Innovation

NOTE: There are four activities to this exercise. They can be conducted all in one session or over several sessions.

Objective: To encourage participants to celebrate their creativity, specifically:

1. **Curiosity** – the ability to find new information without being prompted. Students are encouraged to think creatively about building entrepreneurial ideas.

2. **Self-efficacy** – the belief in one's own innate ability to solve problems and achieve goals.

3. **Autonomy** – the degree to which an individual believes that he or she has control over the outcome of events.

4. **Growth mindset** – the belief that intelligence is not static but can develop throughout life. Students are inspired and energized to look inside themselves for the innovation, creativity and energy that are characteristics of entrepreneurship, the ... "If I think I can, I can!" building of self esteem.

5. **Collaboration** – understanding of 'piggy backing' in self–employment (the value of building on another entrepreneur's idea).

Materials:

o   playing cards
o   bee necklaces
o   paper clips
o   flower forms
o   markers
o   flip chart

Room set-up: Place chairs in groups of six to eight. Each participant in the group is given a flower form, a playing card, a paperclip, and a bee necklace (either all at once or distributed individually just prior to each activity as the teacher/facilitator prefers).

Facilitator script: "Sometimes people believe that they can only think of creative ideas or be successful in entrepreneurship if they have lots of cash, good connections, even the 'right education'. But creativity is within each of us."

PLAYING CARDS ACTIVITY

Facilitator script: "You have been given a playing card. This card is yours to keep. Do you have a low card? A high card? In your group, discuss which card you think is "best?' Who is holding it?"

Facilitator instruction: *Allow conversation for 5 minutes.*

Facilitator script continues: "As an entrepreneur, you have certain assets, talents, and circumstances ... it's not the size of the card, the suit of the card, or the number of the card...it's how you play! In your group, discuss what you think that means."

Facilitator instruction: *Allow conversation for 5 minutes.*

PAPER CLIP ACTIVITY

Facilitator script: "You have been given a paper clip. Look at your paper clip. We all know its traditional usage. Be creative and use the right side of your brain where creative thought is formed.

For example, when I look at this paperclip,

'My paperclip can be used as ....an earring.'

'My paperclip can be used as..........a toothpick.'"

Facilitator instruction: *Go around the room, asking for participation or allow participants to call out their ideas.*

BEE NECKLACE

(NOTE: If you have a challenge sourcing bee necklaces, they are also available through shosholosa.com)

Facilitator script: "You have been given a bee necklace. Look at your bee. Hang the cord over your index finger. Straighten the cord and ensure that the bee is hanging steadily and not moving around. Now tell your brain to tell the nerve ending on your index finger to tell that bee to start swinging from left to right across your body."

Facilitator instruction: *Pause for 30 minutes to allow this to happen.*

Facilitator script continues: "Now stop the bee from swinging and let it hang steady and not move around. Now tell your brain to tell the nerve ending on your index finger to tell that bee to start swinging towards your body and away from your body."

Facilitator instruction: *Pause for 30 seconds to allow this to happen.*

Facilitator script continues: "Now stop the bee from swinging and let it hang steady and not move around. Now tell your brain to tell the nerve ending on your index finger tell that bee to start swinging around in circles."

Facilitator instruction: *Pause for 30 minutes to allow this to happen.*

Facilitator script continues: "Always remind yourself of how powerful you are to 'make things happen."

FLOWER SHAPE

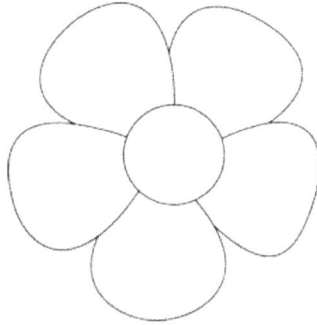

Room set-up: Place participants in groups of four-six students, each with a flower shape.

Facilitator script: "Everyone here has the chance to build their own entrepreneurial venture around a CORE business. This exercise will help you get your creative juices going to picture the multitude of related ideas that can spring up around each and every existing business. Imagine that a garage, selling just gas, is the CORE business represented here in the centre of this flower. What related ventures might benefit through cooperation and interdependence by establishing themselves around the gas being sold at the garage? Imagine that each of the petals around the CORE represents these potential ventures."

Facilitator instruction: *Assign each group a CORE business.*

Facilitator script: "Each group has a different CORE business. HOTEL, GARAGE, SCHOOL GYMNASIUM, GRAIN FARM. Think of the resources and space available in your CORE business and then think creatively of five entrepreneurial ventures that might 'fit' around this CORE—each one represented by one of the petals. Each idea must be somewhat related to the CORE business. For example, a hair salon may fit around a hotel, but is it well suited around a garage? Then again, all those workers may need a haircut!"

Facilitator instruction: *Go around the room, asking for participation or allow participants to call out their ideas.*

EXERCISE 2

The Art of Entrepreneurial Thinking/Perseverance, Resilience, Learning From Mistakes and Setbacks

DON'T LIMIT YOUR
CHALLENGES
CHALLENGE
YOUR LIMITS

Objective: For participants to develop resilience – being able to work through challenges and persist with attempts to achieve one's goal.

Materials:

o   one deck of "Memory" entrepreneurship cards

Room set up:

- Mix up the cards.
- Lay them in rows, face down.

Facilitator instruction: *Students will take turns playing the classic game of "Memory". When a card is flipped, take the opportunity to discuss the quotes with the students.*

Facilitator instruction:

- *Have a student turn over any two cards.*
- *If the two cards match, discuss the quotes with the students in the group, and then set them aside. If the cards don't match, turn them back over.*
- *Students will take turns trying to match cards. The students should watch the play of other students, try to remember what was on each card and where it was located, so when their turn arrives they can match a pair of cards..*
- *The activity is over when all of the cards have been matched.*

Facilitator script after each matching turn: "What does the quote mean to you? How can it relate to business or being an entrepreneur?"

Facilitator instruction: *After the completion of the game, discuss challenges, failures, and opportunities in business.*

EXERCISE 3

*The Art of Intrapreneurial Thinking/*Cooperation and Interdependence Using the Thrive In A Hive Model

Objective: To help participants understand the concept and benefits of intrapreneurship, specifically:

1. **Value creation** – the ability to evaluate the extent to which value can be created for the business and society. Participants are inspired and energized by the idea of creatively constructing an interconnected entrepreneurship system.

2. **Innovation** – the ability to be creative and turn imaginative ideas into reality. Participants gain an understanding and framework of how to analyze the nature of intrapreneurship and what issues are important to cooperation and interdependence.

3. **Collaboration** - participants gain experience in collaboration working with team members by asking for the input of others and by contributing to the ideas of others.

Time required for exercise: 40 minutes

Materials:

- o A table for each group
- o A table cloth for each group that is colour coordinated to their THRIVE IN A HIVE package
- o A pre-packaged THRIVE IN A HIVE kit
- o One animal for every group
- o A display board for each group
- o Prizes

Room set-up: ensure there is a table for each group to work around and that each table has a different coloured tablecloth

Facilitator instructions: *Assign groups of 6 to 8 participants to each table.*

INTRODUCTION OF EXERCISE

Facilitator script: "For this activity you will be working as a team—almost like a hive of bees. You will decide how to work together so consider this an opportunity for you to create your own business community of cooperation and interdependence. The main purpose is to understand *intrapreneurship* which, simply put, is entrepreneurship practised from within a stable and supportive structure of cooperation and *inter*-dependence between participants in a venture.

"Each participant has a different interest, passion, and ability—much like the varied roles and activities that different bees take within a hive. The beehive is the epitome of efficiency; carefully crafted and constructed in a well-designed honeycomb pattern. The hive system has astounded and enchanted the minds of scientists and non-scientists—all of us in fact—for centuries. A close look at the workings of a bee colony, and the goal of preserving the colony and producing honey, gives an analogy for today's ideal organization.

"There is a space and place for many varying roles—including the entrepreneur. Today I want us to use the imagery of the hive to explore our talents, goals and in many ways the interconnectedness that our entrepreneurial projects may take. Instead of thinking of yourself as an entrepreneur working alone or with a partner—think of yourself as an entrepreneur working and 'thriving in a hive.'"

EXPLANATION OF EXERCISE

Facilitator script: "Imagine that you and everyone else in your group has a paid job in a zoo. In each group, there is a CORE zoo animal. The zoo pays you to look after the zoo animal but in your spare time you are able to be an *intra*preneur and think creatively about business ventures that can develop around your animal. If your zoo animal is a *sheep*, for example, you are paid to keep the sheep at the CORE healthy, watered, sheltered and fed so that visitors to the zoo pay to come in and look at the *sheep*. But what business ventures can grow up around a *sheep*?"

Facilitator instruction: *Gather from the students their "obvious" ideas (e.g. wool/clothing/meat industry) then add the true story of a zoo that is making money selling Zoo Poo as gardening soil.*

Facilitator script: "As of 2021, Zoo Poo was a commodity being sold at the gift shop at the Dallas Zoo. It is exactly what it sounds like. Animal poop, processed and sold as planting soil. It is reportedly part of the Dallas' Zoo's push for sustainability. As well as the Dallas Zoo's gift shop, local specialty stores also carry it. The recycling company, Silver Creek Materials, partnered with the Dallas Zoo to turn elephants, giraffes, hippos, and other herbivores' manure into compost.

"How about a clothing line of "Black Sheep T-shirts?"

Facilitator instruction: *Distribute the packages of materials used to represent business ideas: coloured tablecloth, display board, and an animal for the group to use as their core zoo animal. Ensure each group has sufficient space to move around and construct display.*

Facilitator script: "The materials in the kit should help provide inspiration for you to create your proposed new ventures. Put your animal on your display board as the CORE. Work together as a group to brainstorm all the creative ideas that might make you money surrounding the theme of your zoo animal. This is similar to the flower form activity we did (name the date if this exercise was used previously).

"This is a time for you to think creatively as intrapreneurs. There is no risk. If your ideas don't make money—you still have your job looking after the sheep!

"You can work alone on an idea that you think will make money, or in pairs or in your larger group. Just work on the ideas that YOU feel passionate about. Work on developing the sections of the display where you have the most interest. You can use anything to represent your ideas. That's what entrepreneurs do!"

Facilitator instruction: *Facilitate brainstorming.*

Facilitator script: "Divide into individuals, pairs, triads, foursomes, etc. and work on developing the section or sections of the display where you have an interest. Offer suggestions if and when your group members ask. Collaborate ... that's what intrapreneurs do!"

Facilitator instruction: *Debrief.*

EXERCISE 4

The Art of Intrapreneurial Thinking/Core Expenses and Tasks Using the Thrive In A Hive Model

Objective: For participants to develop an understanding of possible entrepreneurial careers/paths, with the possible following outcomes.

Participants learn to:

1. How to cluster a series of related businesses

2. How to make judgments on the feasibility of ventures

3. How to evaluate an opportunity – i.e. the ability to evaluate and decide about an opportunity by seeing links between unrelated pieces of information

4. Develop creative problem solving – the ability to identify, redefine and create opportunity out of problems. Understand that entrepreneurship is an organic process of "trial and error" learning

5. Become action orientated – willing to take practical action to deal with a problem, without being prompted

6. Develop leadership – the ability to lead a group of people to achieve an overarching vision while holding each individual accountable for their performance.

Materials:

o   Entrepreneurial idea boards from Exercise 3 (The Art of Intrapreneurial Thinking/Cooperation and Interdependence Using the Thrive In A Hive Model)
o   Paper, markers for each group

INTRODUCTION

Facilitator instructions: *Ensure that each group can see the display boards from Exercise 3, and have paper, markers*

Facilitator script: "Let's use the analogy of a racehorse to demonstrate the relationship of cooperation and interdependence between a CORE business and the associated 'petal' ventures. It benefits no one to chop up the racehorse into little pieces and give each person a piece. However, if the racehorse in the CORE stays healthy, the 'petals' can benefit.

"For example, one person takes the responsibility of feeding and watering the animal, another takes on the task of exercising it, another sees to its medical needs, and one trains it for race day. The CORE business continues to 'own' the racehorse. It is the ownership of this racehorse that motivates some people to become entrepreneurial and some entrepreneurs to generate the economic activity that can provide economic opportunities to others. A participant in a collaborative project like this may choose to provide exercise services to other horses, dogs, and pet goats while at the same time developing expertise with racehorses.

"That becomes his or her personal enterprise, and he or she reaps the full benefit of that labour. That person's efforts may very well attract customers who are also interested in the services of a horse feed expert and thereby become customers of those involved in tending the racehorse. But the racehorse must never be neglected because it is the CORE racehorse making all the other enterprises possible. There must always be a clear understanding that the CORE business, the 'Queen Bee' —in this case, the racehorse— is there for the benefit of all, and that the effort each individual invests in their business must in some way enhance the performance of the racehorse, the 'Queen Bee' of the hive, therefore benefitting all other participants. Each business is stronger through the wholehearted participation of each of the others.

"If you were in charge of building Intrapreneurship—which of the ideas in front of you would you think have the best chance of growing into self-sufficient units? On these blank display boards or pieces of paper, draw or illustrate the ideas that might have the best chance to grow. Don't eliminate any ideas."

Activity A

Facilitator instruction: *Give participants time to complete discussion and put ideas on paper/display boards.*

Facilitator script: "Next, discuss what costs or infrastructure might be required?"

Facilitator instruction: *Give participants time to complete discussion and put ideas on paper/display boards.*

Facilitator instruction: *Debrief.*

Activity B

Facilitator script: "Now look around at ALL the projects in the room and determine which ideas in the whole room could be linked? For example, can all the animal rides concepts be combined? Talk together and see what might emerge if each of the sections of the zoo start to collaborate."

Facilitator instruction: *Debrief.*

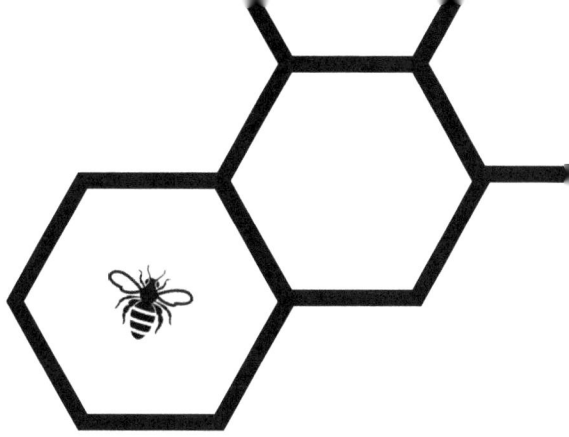

EXERCISE 5

Entrepreneurial Process Elements/ Options for Business Structures

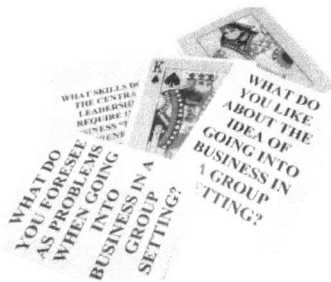

Objective:

For participants to examine the benefits of working alone, with a partner, or with others through cooperation and inter-dependence. Activities compare and contrast entrepreneurship and intrapreneurship and explore constraints to innovation within organizations.

Possible outcomes:

1. Participants are familiarized with all structural options for entrepreneurship. Sole proprietor? Small or large partnership? Intrapreneurship?

2. Participants gain experience in an oral communication style of "talking in circles"

Time required for exercise: 40 minutes

Room set-up: participants should be in groups of 4.
Music is optional for this exercise.

Materials:

- o   Markers
- o   Flip Chart
- o   Sets of four playing cards
- o   Matrix guide for each participant
- o   Talking sticks
- o   Introduction

Facilitator instruction: *Form participant groups of four. Each participant in the group is given a card: with one each of ACE, KING, QUEEN, JACK. If the participant group does not neatly break down into groups of four, give a JOKER card to any unassigned participants.. JOKERS are NOT in a group of four – and these participants are free to roam between groups and participate in any conversation.*

Each of the FOUR face cards has a different question:

ACE: *What do you like about the idea of going into business in a group setting?*

KING: *What do you foresee as problems when going into business in a group setting?*

QUEEN: *What do you see as problems going into business alone? In a small partnership?*

JACK: *What do you like about going into business alone or in a small partnership?*

JOKERS *may roam!*

Activity A

Facilitator instructions: *Use the Matrix chart to show participants how to keep moving within the group until everyone has answered everyone else's questions.*

Facilitator script: "You now each have a card with a question and character. This is the question you will ask of the rest of your group of four. Let me guide you through the matrix process. In the first round, ACES and KINGS sit together; ACE asks the question, KING answers. QUEENS and JACKS sit together; QUEEN asks the question, JACK answers."

Facilitator instruction: *Allow five minutes for this round of the activity.*

Facilitator script: "In the second round, KINGS and QUEENS sit together; KING asks the question, QUEEN answers. JACKS and

ACES sit together; JACK asks the question, ACE answers."

Facilitator instruction: *Allow five minutes for the activity.*

Facilitator script: "In the third round, ACES and QUEENS sit together; ACE asks the question, QUEEN answers. KINGS and JACKS sit together; KING asks the question, JACK answers."

Facilitator instruction: *Allow five minutes for this round of the activity.*

Facilitator script: "In the Fourth round, QUEENS and KINGS sit together; QUEEN asks the question, KING answers. ACES and JACKS sit together; ACE asks the question, JACK answers."

Facilitator instruction: *Allow five minutes for this round of the activity.*

Facilitator script: "In the fifth round, KINGS and ACES sit together; KING asks the question, ACE answers. JACKS and QUEENS sit together; JACK asks the question, QUEEN answers."

Facilitator instruction: *Allow five minutes for this round of the activity.*

Facilitator script: "In the sixth round, QUEENS & ACES sit together; QUEEN asks the question, ACE answers. JACKS and KINGS sit together, JACK asks the question, KING answers ."

Facilitator instruction: *Ask participants to share their feedback and insights.*

Activity B

Facilitator instructions: *Form groups of all Aces, all Kings, all Queens, and all Jacks. Give each group a talking stick. Jokers to sit with whichever group they choose.*

Facilitator script: "In each circle, one participant at a time will hold the talking stick and gives a summary of the answers they heard to the question asked on their card."

Facilitator instruction: *Give appropriate time for the activity.*

Facilitator script: "Pick one person to best summarize the ideas heard in your group. This is our 'collective wisdom' gathered by this process."

Facilitator instruction: *Write down summary points on flip chart.*

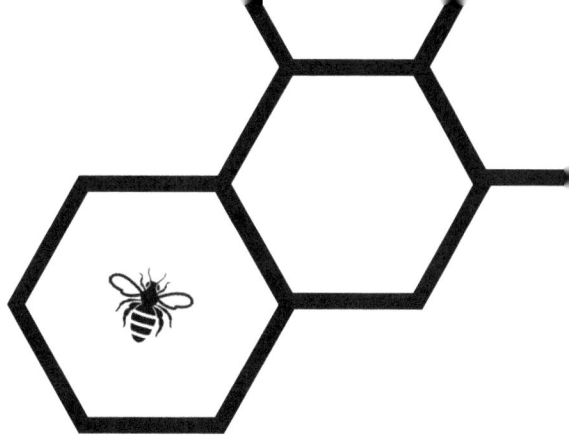

EXERCISE 6

Entrepreneurial Process Elements/Branding

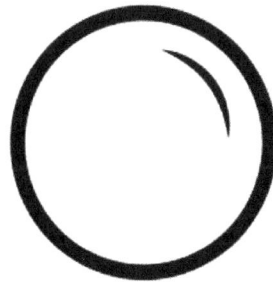

Objective: Participants explore the impact of marketing and branding efforts.

Possible outcomes:

1. Students gain an understanding of the links between their values and those of others.

2. Students gain an understanding of a framework to display their collaborative individualism and ideas.

Materials:

- o Identical white ping pong balls – one ball per group
- o Identical plastic lemon/fresh lemon – one per group

Facilitator instructions: *Distribute the balls, one to each group. Have them inspect the balls and then return them to the pile.*

Facilitator script: "Can you identify your ball in the basket with the other balls."

Facilitator instructions: *The students will be unable to distinguish their individual ball in the basket. This is to show that the balls are all the same and branding is required to create differentiation.*

Facilitator script: "Branding is more than a logo or advertising strategy. It is your reputation, your unique identity that sets you and your business apart from your competition.

"It is an emotional connection between a company, product, or service and the customer. It is a promise of value. It is what people buy when they buy your product or service. A brand must have meaning to its consumers and to its employees.

"It is based on a promise—what the brand says it will do to help the customer. It is also the customer's perception of the product or service, their overall experience of the brand.

"The challenge is to define, implement and manage your reputation so it says what you want it to say.

"In a world where one's competitors are only a phone call or a mouse click away, standing out from the competition is increasingly important. Businesses must stand out in a distinctive way and ensure that everything between them and the client/customer communicates the same message.

Facilitator instructions: *Distribute the white balls, one per group.*

Facilitator script: "Customize your white ball to brand it."

Facilitator instructions: *Give the group time to customize their ball.*

Facilitator script: "Here are some considerations:

1. think beyond visuals
2. make it something others cannot copy
3. keep it narrowly focused
4. be certain it is accurate and defendable
5. keep your image and materials current and tailored to your public
6. if you use design a brand name, make it short, simple, and memorable."

Facilitator instructions: *Distribute the lemons, one per group.*

Facilitator script: "Keeping in mind the branding you have already done for the ball, how would further develop/explain your brand by using the lemon. Customize your lemon to brand it. Remember the considerations we discussed earlier:

- think beyond visuals
- make it something others cannot copy
- keep it narrowly focused
- be certain it is accurate and defendable
- keep your image and materials current and tailored to your public
- if you use design a brand name, make it short, simple, and memorable."

Facilitator instructions: *Give the group time to customize their lemon.*

Facilitator instructions: *Debrief.*

References

3M Company. (2002). *A century of innovation: The 3M story.* Retrieved from http://multimedia.3m.com/mws/media/171240O/3m-coi-book-tif.pdf

Adcroft, A., Willis, R., & Dhaliwal, S. (2004). Missing the point? Management education and entrepreneurship. *Management Decision, 42*(3/4), 512–521. https://dx.doi.org/10.1108/00251740410518958

All in the Mind: A different breed of manager. (2009). The *Economist, 390*(8622), 4.

Anderson, M., Galloway, L., Brown, L., & Wilson, L. (2003). *Skills development for the modern economy.* Paper presented at the 23rd ISBA National Small Firms Conference, Guildford, United Kingdom.

Anselm, M. (1993). *Entrepreneurship education in the community college.* Paper presented at the 38th International Council for Small Business (ICSB): Entrepreneurship Education in the Community College, Las Vegas, NV.

Audretsch, D. (2004). Sustaining innovation and growth: Public policy support for entrepreneurship. *Industry and Innovation, 11*(3), 167–191.

Audretsch, D., Thurik, R., Verheul, I., & Wennekers, S. (Eds.). (2002). *Entrepreneurship: Determinants and policy in a European–US comparison.* Boston, MA: Kluwer.

Burgelman, R. A. (1983). A process model of internal corporate venturing in the diversified major firm. *Administrative Science Quarterly, 28*(2), 223–244. https://dx.doi.org/10.2307/2392619

Burgelman, R. A. (1988). Managing the internal corporate venturing process. In M. L. Tushman & W. L. Moore (Eds.), *Readings in the management of innovation* (pp. 585–602). Boston, MA: Ballinger.

Busenitz, L. W., West, G. P., III, Shepherd, D., Nelson, T., Chandler, G. N., & Zacharakis, A. (2003). Entrepreneurship research in emergence: Past trends and future direction. *Journal of Management, 29*(3), 285–308. https://dx.doi.org/10.1016/S0149-2063(03)00013-8

Butler, J. (2003). *Risk and failure as "lifelong learning": Entrepreneurship training programs in Saskatchewan and the state promotion of "Me, Inc."* (Unpublished doctoral thesis). Saskatoon, University of Saskatchewan.

Caree, M. A., & Thurik, A. R. (2010). The impact of entrepreneurship on economic growth. In Z. J. Acs & D. B. Audretsch (Eds.), *The handbook of entrepreneurship research* (pp. 557–594). New York, NY: Springer.

Casson, M. (2000). Entrepreneurship and the theory of the firm. In Z. A. Acs, C. Carlsson, & C. Karlsson (Eds.), *Entrepreneurship in small and medium sized enterprises and the macro economy* (pp. 45–78). Cambridge, United Kingdom: Cambridge University Press.

Chaharbaghi, K., & Willis, R. (2000). The technology, mythology and economy of technology. *Management Decision, 38*(6), 394–402. https://dx.doi.org/10.1108/00251740010344577

Commission of the European Communities. (2003, January). *Green paper: Entrepreneurship in Europe.* Retrieved from http://ec.europa.eu/invest-in-research/pdf/download_en/entrepreneurship_europe.pdf

Community Futures Saskatchewan. (2003). *Taking care of business.* Retrieved from https://cfsask.ca/images/newsask/pdfs/Newsask_Teacher_Guide.pdf

Coneys, M. (2003). *Dance to the beat of your own drum.* Regina, Canada: Author.

Coneys, M. (2005). Intrapreneurship: A development step toward successful business ventures by women (Master's thesis). Available from ProQuest Dissertations and Theses database. (UMI No. MR04171)

Davidsson, P. (2005). *Researching entrepreneurship.* Berlin, Germany: Springer.

Deamer, I., & Earle, L. (2004). Searching for entrepreneurship. *Industrial and Commercial Training, 36*(3), 99–103. https://dx.doi.org/10.1108/00197850410532096

Dewey, J. (1910). *How we think.* New York, NY: D. C. Heath.

Dewey, J. (1916). *Democracy and education*. New York, NY: Free Press.

Drucker, P. F. (1985). *Innovation and entrepreneurship.* New York, NY: Harper & Row.

Entrepreneurship. (2009, April 27). *The Economist.* Retrieved from http://www.economist.com/node/13565718

Ernst & Young. (2009). *Entrepreneurship and innovation: The keys to global economic recovery* (White Paper). London, United Kingdom:

Falkäng, J., & Alberti, F. (2000). The assessment of entrepreneurship education. *Industry and Higher Education, 14*(2), 101–108. https://dx.doi.org/10.5367/000000000101294931

Fiet, J. O. (200la). The pedagogical side of entrepreneurship theory. *Journal of Business Venturing, 16*(2), 101–117. https://dx.doi.org/10.1016/S0883-9026(99)00042-7

Fiet, J. O. (2001b). The theoretical side of teaching entrepreneurship. *Journal of Business Venturing, 16*(1), 1–24. https://dx.doi.org/10.1016/S0883-9026(99)00041-5

Galloway, L., & Brown, W. (2002). Entrepreneurship education at university: A driver in the creation of high growth firms. *Education + Training, 44*(8/9), 398–405. https://dx.doi.org/10.1108/00400910210449231

Gibb, A. A. (1993). The enterprise culture and education: Understanding enterprise education and its links with small business, entrepreneurship and wider educational goals. *International Small Business Management Journal, 11*(3), 1–34. https://dx.doi.org/10.1177/026624269301100301

Gorman, G., Hanlon, D., & King, W. (1997). Some research perspectives on entrepreneurship education, enterprise education, and education for small business management: A ten-year literature review. *International Small Business Journal, 15*, 56–77.

Government of Norway. (2010). *Action plan: Entrepreneurship in education and training – from compulsory school to higher education 2009–2014.* Retrieved from https://www.regjeringen.no/globalassets/documents/action-plan-for-entrepreneurship-in-education-and-training-2009.pdf

Greene, P. G., Katz, J. A., & Johannisson, B. (2004). Entrepreneurship education (editorial). *The Academy of Management Learning & Education, 3*(3), 238–241. https://dx.doi.org/10.5465/AMLE.2004.14242093

Hytti, U., & O'Gorman, C. (2004). What is "enterprise education"? An analysis of the objectives and methods of enterprise education programmes in four countries. *Education and Training, 46*(1), 11–23. https://dx.doi.org/10.1108/00400910410518188

Ihde, D. (1990). *Technology and the lifeworld: From garden to earth.* Bloomington, IN: Indiana University Press.

Institute for Defense Analyses. (n.d.). *Science and Technology Policy Institute (STPI).* Retrieved from https://www.ida.org/stpi.php

Intrapreneur. (n.d.). In *The American heritage dictionary.* Retrieved from https://www.ahdictionary.com/word/search.html?q=intrapreneur

Jack, S. L., & Anderson, A. R. (1999). Entrepreneurship education within the enterprise culture: Producing reflective practitioners. *International Journal of Entrepreneurial Behaviour & Research, 5*(3), 110–125. https://dx.doi.org/10.1108/13552559910284074

Junior Achievement Canada. (n.d.). *JA Canada.* Retrieved from http://jacanada.org/

Junior Achievement Eurpoe. (n.d.). *JA Europe.* Retrieved from http://www.jaeurope.org/

Junior Achievement Young Enterprise Norway. (2009). *JA-YE Norway.* Retrieved from http://www.create2009.europa.eu/fileadmin/Content/Downloads/PDF/Projects/National_projects/NO_JA_YE.pdf

Katz, J. A. (2003). The chronology and intellectual trajectory of American entrepreneurship education. In *Entrepreneurship Education.* New York, NY: Quorum Books.

Kaufman-RAND Institute. (n.d.). *Kauffman-RAND Institute for Entrepreneurship Public Policy: Studying the way legal and regulatory policymaking affect small businesses and entrepreneurship.* Retrieved from https://www.rand.org/jie/science-technology-policy/centers/entrepreneurship.html

Kolb, D. (1984). *Experiential learning: Experience at the source of learning and development.* Englewood Cliffs, NJ: Prentice-Hall.

Kuratko, D. F. (2003). *Entrepreneurship education: Emerging trends and challenges for the 21st century* (White Paper Series). Chicago, IL: Coleman Foundation.

Kuratko, D. F. (2004). *Entrepreneurship education in the 21st century: From legitimization to leadership* (White Paper). Retrieved from http://faculty.bus.olemiss.edu/dhawley/PMBA622%20SP07/PMBA622/Sloan/L3_M11_Entre_Education.pdf

Kuratko, D. F. (2005). The emergence of entrepreneurship education: Development, trends, and challenges. *Entrepreneurship: Theory and Practice, 29*(5), 577–598. https://dx.doi.org/10.1111/j.1540-6520.2005.00099.x

Kuratko, D. F. (2014). *Entrepreneurship: Theory, process, practice* (9th ed.). Mason, OH: Cengage/Southwestern.

Kuratko, D. F., & Hodgetts, R. M. (2004). *Entrepreneurship: Theory, process, practice*. Mason, OH: South-Western.

Laverty, S. M. (2003). Hermeneutic phenomenology and phenomenology: A comparison of historical and methodological considerations. *International Journal of Qualitative Methods, 2*(3), 21–35. https://dx.doi.org/10.1177/160940690300200303

Luckner, J. L., & Nadler, R. S. (1997). *Processing the experience.* Dubuque, IA: Kendall/Hunt.

Lüthje, C., & Franke, N. (2002). *Fostering entrepreneurship through university education and training: Lessons from Massachusetts Institute of Technology.* European Academy of Management 2nd Annual Conference on Innovative Research in Management, Stockholm, Sweden.

Martin, B. C., McNally, J. J., & Kay, M. J. (2013). Examining the formation of human capital in entrepreneurship: A meta-analysis of entrepreneurship education outcomes. *Journal of Business Venturing, 28*(2), 211–224. https://dx.doi.org/10.1016/j.jbusvent.2012.03.002

McKeown, J., Millman, C., Sursani, S. R., Smith, K., & Martin, L. M. (2006). *UK graduate entrepreneurship education in England, Wales and Scotland* (National Council for Graduate Entrepreneurship Working Paper Series). Retrieved from http://www.ncge.org.uk/

Mitchell, R. K., Busenitz, L., Lant, T., McDougall, P. P., Morse, E. A., & Smith, J. B. (2002). Toward a theory of entrepreneurial cognition: Rethinking the people side of entrepreneurship research. *Entrepreneurship Theory and Practice, 26*(4), 93–104. https://dx.doi.org/10.1111/1540-8520.00001

The National Centre for Social Entrepreneurs. (n.d.). *Welcome to the world of possibilities.* Retrieved from https://nationalcenterforsocialentrepreneurs.wordpress.com/

The National Consortium for Entrepreneurship Education. (n.d.-a). *About us... EntreEd*. Retrieved from http://www.entre-ed.org/about/

The National Consortium for Entrepreneurship Education. (n.d.-b). *Curriculum – examples*. Retrieved from http://www.entreed.org/Standards_Toolkit/curriculum_examples.htm

National Content Standards for Entrepreneurial Education. (n.d.). *About the consortium for entrepreneurial education*. Retrieved from http://www.entreed.org/Standards_Toolkit/about_cee.htm

Neck, H. M., & Greene, P. G. (2011). Known worlds and new frontiers. *Journal of Small Business Management, 49*(1), 55–70. https://dx.doi.org/10.1111/j.1540-627X.2010.00314.x

Nieuwenhuizen, C., & Groenwald, D. (2004). *Entrepreneurship training and education needs as determined by the brain preference profiles of successful, established entrepreneurs.* Paper presented at the Internationalising Entrepreneurship Education and Training, Naples, FL.

O'Connor, A. (2009). *Enterprise, education and economic development: An exploration of entrepreneurship's economic function in the Australian government's education policy* (Doctoral dissertation). Swinburne University of Technology, Melbourne, Australia.

O'Connor, A., & Yamin, S. (2011). Innovation and entrepreneurship: Managing the paradox of purpose in business model innovation. *International Journal of Learning and Intellectual Capital, 8*(3), 239–255. https://dx.doi.org/10.1504/IJLIC.2011.041071

Organisation for Economic Co-operation and Development. (2011). *Skills for innovation and research.* Retrieved from http://www.oecd-ilibrary.org/docserver/download/9789264097490-sum-en.pdf

Payne, P. (1994). Restructuring the discursive moral subject in ecological feminism. In K. J. Warren (Ed.), *Ecological feminism* (pp. 139–157). London, United Kingdom: Routledge.

Payne, P. (1995). Ontology and the critical discourse of environmental education. The Australian Journal of Environmental Education, 11, 83–105.

Payne, P. (1996). Technology, phenomenology and educational inquiry. *Australian Educational Researcher*, 23(3), 81–95.

Payne, P. (2005). Ways of doing: Learning, teaching and researching coherence, congruence and commensurability. *Canadian Journal of Environmental Education, 10*(1), 108–124.

Peterman, N. E., & Kennedy, J. (2003). Enterprise education: Influencing students' perceptions of entrepreneurship. *Entrepreneurship Theory and Practice, 28*(2), 129–144.

Pinchot, G. (1986). *Intrapreneuring: Why you don't have to leave the corporation to become an entrepreneur.* New York, NY: Harper & Row.

Pittaway, L. A. (2004). *Simulating entrepreneurial learning: Accessing the utility of experiential learning designs* (Entrepreneurship and Enterprise Development Working Paper Series). Lancaster, United Kingdom: Institute for Entrepreneurship and Enterprise Development, Lancaster University.

Pittaway, L., & Cope, J. (2007). Entrepreneurship education: A systematic review of the evidence. *International Small Business Journal, 25*(5), 479–510.

Rushing, F. W., & Kent, C. A. (2000). The status of entrepreneurship education in elementary and secondary schools in the United States. In D. Lines (Ed.), *Effective strategies in economics and business education: An international perspective* (pp. 1–163). London, United Kingdom: The Economics and Business Education Association.

Saskatchewan Learning. (2004). *Entrepreneurship 30 curriculum guide: A practical and applied art.* Retrieved from http://publications.gov. sk.ca/documents/11/40538-Entrepreneurship_30_2004.pdf

Scarborough, N., & Cornwall, J. (2016). *Essentials of entrepreneurship and small business management* (8th ed.). Englewood Cliffs, NJ: Pearson/ Prentice-Hall.

Schumpeter, J. A. (1934). *The theory of economic development.* Cambridge, MA: Harvard University Press.

Schumpeter, J. A. (1961). *History of economic analysis.* New York, NY: Oxford University Press.

Wang, C. K., Wong, P. K., & Lu, Q. (2001, June). *Entrepreneurial intentions and tertiary education.* Conference on Technological Entrepreneurship in the Emerging Regions of the New Millennium, Singapore./

Young, J. E. (1997). Entrepreneurship education and learning for university students and practicing entrepreneurs. In D. L. Sexton & R. W. Smilor (Eds.), *Entrepreneurship 2000.* Chicago, IL: Upstart.

Author Biography

Dr. Monica Knight is an entrepreneur, speaker, facilitator, motivator, teacher, and consultant whose career path has taken her from Europe to India and Africa and finally to Canada, where she a Professor at the Faculty of Management at Vancouver Island University. Monica holds a Ph.D. from the University of Regina, Saskatchewan, a Master in Leadership and Training from Royal Roads in Victoria, British Columbia, and a Diploma in Education, Liverpool, United Kingdom.

In addition to her role in academia, Monica is a keynote speaker through her firm, *Shosholoza! EDUtainment*. Monica's spirit is unique and avant garde and her wisdom is presented through music, dance, and humour. A sought-after EDUtainer (presenting education as entertainment), she inspires, challenges, and encourages others to release their own right-brained caged bird and hold on tightly for a magical roller coaster ride to entrepreneurial success.

Dr. Knight's toolkit and examples foster an entrepreneurial spirit and stimulate entrepreneurial initiatives. She facilitates creative and innovative collaboration with those desiring to build their entrepreneurial capacity. Those who follow her philosophy and utilize her *Thrive in a Hive* toolkit easily learn that they too can be enterprising wherever they exercise confidence and self-reliance.

Working With Monica

Are you interested in having Monica present the advanced exercises to your group?

To speak at your upcoming event?

To work with your community?

Contact Monica at:

Monica Knight, PhD
Marmalade Cottage and Ubuntu House
2-3 755 Church Street
Gabriola Island, British Columbia
V0R 1X3

Email: monica@shosholoza.ca
Cell: 250-802-4313

Shosholoza!
EDUtainment Keynotes & Workshops

www.ingramcontent.com/pod-product-compliance
Lightning Source LLC
Chambersburg PA
CBHW062042200326
41519CB00017B/5112